CHRIST'S VICTORIOUS CHURCH

Christ's Victorious Church

Essays on Biblical Ecclesiology and Eschatology in Honor of Tom Friskney

Edited by

Jon A. Weatherly

Wipf and Stock Publishers
150 West Broadway • Eugene OR 97401
2001

Christ's Victorious Church: Essays on Biblical Ecclesiology and Eschatology in Honor of Tom Friskney

Edited by Jon A. Weatherly

ISBN: 1-57910-738-9

Printed by *Wipf and Stock Publishers*
150 West Broadway • Eugene OR 97401

Contents

Preface

Festschrift is a German word that refers to a collection of academic essays written and published to honor a significant, senior member of the academic community at an important milestone, usually a retirement, and focusing on the academic subject that especially interested the person honored. By that description, this book is *mostly* a Festschrift.

It is a collection of mostly academic essays. Most are written by professors. But some of those professors contributed essays that are deliberately more homiletic than academic. One contributor spent his career in local-church ministry, but his essay is scholarly. Another contributor, whom publishers would characterize as "an informed, thoughtful lay person," writes a reflective and personal essay on a subject of academic theology. These are not the usual elements of a Festschrift, but they appropriately echo the honoree's own wide-ranging voice.

This book is written to honor someone who is mostly a significant, senior member of the academic community, but who is also much more. To all who know Cincinnati Bible College and Seminary (CBC&S) and to many in the independent Christian churches and churches of Christ, Tom Friskney is most familiar as the long-time Professor of New Testament and Greek at CBC&S. However, during his academic tenure he was just as busy as a preacher as he was as a college professor, pursuing both vocations at a pace well beyond what most would consider "full time." Furthermore, his academic contribution is best measured less by the common scale of academic publications (though publish he did) and more by the deep influence that he had on the students whom he taught. This volume's contributors, whose range of professions reflect the varied career of the one celebrated, represent a fraction of the students and colleagues whose approach to the Bible was profoundly shaped by Tom Friskney. His significance as a scholar is reflected in the lives of the many students who teach in colleges and seminaries and preach in churches with the unmistakable marks of his influence.

This book is presented mostly, or at least approximately, for an important milestone in the honoree's career. In keeping with the pace of his working life, Tom Friskney's retirement has been anything but idle. After his formal retirement, he continued to teach part-time at CBC&S. Having only recently ended his classroom teaching altogether, he continues with distance education courses, not to mention a hectic round of commitments in the church and parachurch. So it has been difficult to tie the appearance of this volume to his retirement, a circumstance to which the contributors and editor appeal to excuse our delay in finishing our work.

The themes of this collection reflect two prominent themes in Tom Friskney's teaching: ecclesiology, or the church, and eschatology, or the last things. Those who took his courses or read his books on 1 Corinthians and Revelation will know that his interest in those New Testament books parallels his interest in those subjects. They will also know that he always sought to link these two "-ologies" together. After the introductory biographical essay, this collection is divided into two sections devoted to these two topics, (chapters 2–5 and 6–13 respectively). But that division, in keeping with the Tom's convictions, is somewhat arbitrary. Readers will find much eschatology in the ecclesiology, and vice versa. The overlap of the contributions reminds me of one of Tom Friskney's maxims: "If you want to know what heaven will be like, you have to understand the church." Our hope as contributors and editors is that readers will have further cause to reflect on such truths because of these essays.

Thanks are due to several people for their assistance in bringing this project to completion. Cincinnati Bible College and Seminary and its president, Dr. David Grubbs, have encouraged and underwritten this project from the beginning. All of the contributors are to be thanked for their work in producing their essays and their patience in waiting for the collection to be published. Special thanks are due to Paul Friskney, who provided invaluable advice on the planning of the volume. My administrative assistant Julie Martin supplied a careful eye in the final proofreading. Errors that remain are my responsibility. Minta Berry of SetTingPace, Inc., graciously offered advice on the details of publication. Jim Tedrick of Wipf & Stock Publishers provided superb service in the book's production and distribution. All these have made it possible to present this volume to Tom Friskney with our respect and affection.

JON A. WEATHERLY
July 17, 2001

Contributors

Jack Cottrell is Professor of Theology at Cincinnati Bible College and Seminary (CBC&S). He holds degrees from CBC&S, the University of Cincinnati, Westminster Theological Seminary, and the PhD from Princeton Theological Seminary.

David A. Fiensey is Professor of New Testament at Kentucky Christian College. A graduate of CBC&S, he earned the MA in classics from Xavier University and the PhD in New Testament from Duke University.

Paul Friskney is Associate Professor of English at CBC&S. He holds the BA and MA degrees from CBC&S and the MA from the University of Louisville.

Dennis Gaertner is Professor of New Testament at Johnson Bible College. A graduate of Great Lakes Christian College and CBC&S, he holds the PhD from Southern Baptist Theological Seminary. Prior to joining the faculty at Johnson, he served as Associate Professor of New Testament at CBC&S.

Steve Hooks is Professor of Old Testament at Atlanta Christian College, having previously taught at CBC&S. An Atlanta Christian College alumnus, he received the MDiv from Emmanuel School of Religion and the PhD from Hebrew Union College.

Brian Johnson is Associate Professor of Bible at Lincoln Christian College. He holds the BA and MA degrees from CBC&S and is completing his PhD thesis for the University of Aberdeen.

Charles A. Lee, or "Chuck," holds bachelor's and master's degrees from CBC&S. He is recently retired from the position of Minister of Adult Education at the Southeast Christian Church in Louisville, Kentucky.

Larry Pechawer is Professor of Old Testament at Ozark Christian College. A CBC&S graduate, he did postgraduate studies at Hebrew Union College and served as a professor at CBC&S and as academic dean at Central Christian College of the Bible.

Amanda Smith is an alumna of the undergraduate division of CBC&S. A full-time wife and mother, she also serves as International Student Services Coordinator at CBC&S.

James A. Smith is Associate Professor of Biblical Studies at CBC&S. He received bachelor's and master's degrees from CBC&S and the PhD from the University of Sheffield.

Tom Thatcher is Associate Professor of Biblical Studies at CBC&S. He holds college and seminary degrees from CBC&S and the PhD from Southern Baptist Theological Seminary.

Virgil Warren ministers with the Vermitten (Kansas) Christian Church and is an adjunct instructor at Kansas State University. A former professor at Manhattan Christian College and CBC&S, he earned undergraduate degrees from CBC&S, master's degrees from Wheaton College Graduate School and the PhD from Southern Baptist Theological Seminary.

Jon A. Weatherly is Academic Dean of the College and Professor of New Testament at CBC&S. A graduate of CBC&S, he also received the MDiv from Trinity Evangelical Divinity School and the PhD from the University of Aberdeen.

CHAPTER 1

A Man for All Reasons: A Biographical Essay

PAUL FRISKNEY

My mission, as I have decided to accept it, is to write a biographical essay on my father, Tom Friskney. In many ways, I guess that I am quite qualified for the task. After all, my baby book points out that he was my first visitor in the hospital when I was born. (Back then, fathers were visitors and not participants.) He preached the first sermon I ever heard as well as the first one I remember. He gave me my first paying job (killing potato bugs at a penny each). He taught the first college class in which I ever enrolled (freshman English at 7 a.m.). He even performed the wedding ceremony when my wife and I were married (as he did for my five siblings and their spouses). In fact, now having passed 40, I only recently stopped being introduced as Tom Friskney's son on a regular basis.

Still, there are large portions of Dad's life that I know only a little about. I doubt that it surprises anyone to know that he never talked much about himself. Oh, there were a few famous stories from his childhood: at age 10 when his appendix burst and his life was narrowly saved by an operation, the day in the fields when he got a hayseed in his eye, a mishap that eventually led to legal blindness in that eye. Beyond things like that, I only know the high points: enlisting in the army at 17 and serving in the occupation forces in Japan, marrying my mother, beginning as a farmer before he followed his true calling into ministry.

No, I would be a poor biographer. Hence my mission to write a biographical essay rather than a true biography. Perhaps, that's the only appropriate way to address the life of Tom Friskney. Anyone who has heard him preach or teach about Revelation knows that he's skeptical of time lines and chronologies anyway. His funeral sermons also show his preferences. My dad performs better funerals than anyone else I know. Granted, he has performed more than most, but he has a gift for it. While he carefully researches so that he can write an accurate, brief history of the person's life, his funerals really come alive (pun intended) in the sermons. He captures the essence of who the person is (not was) and what it was like to spend time with him or her. That's what I want to do in this essay.

Let no man say he truly knows my father who hasn't spent time with him in the garden. He loves to work the earth and to watch things grow from it. The care of his gardens and the harvesting of the fruits of his labors bring him great joy. He especially enjoys sharing his flowers with others. In fact, his joy in gardening is so great that he cannot fathom that others do not find it equally rapturous. My father and I fought more in the garden than anywhere else. If you would join your voice with the many who have said to me, "I can't imagine your dad ever raising his voice," let me tell you about the garden.

It wasn't until many years later that I figured out just what the garden meant to Dad. For him, it was both a connection to his heritage and a fundamental illustration of reliance on God. He's quick to say that his childhood on a farm taught him his work ethic and the enjoyment of the simple life. From his own gardening, the produce he generated helped to feed his family when money was very tight, answering the objections of his own father, who told him that he would starve to death as a preacher. The physical labor also relieved his mind and body from the stress of the other activities of his life and continues to keep him so physically fit that he can easily outwork either of his sons and any of his sons-in-law.

While I didn't always realize it, another essential aspect of my dad is his love for family. My parents are the proverbial "match made in heaven." Many times when I have heard critics complain that television shows from the fifties and sixties portrayed an overly simplified, unrealistic view of the marital relationship, I have smiled thinking about the fact that those couples fought more often than my parents. In fact, although I wasn't present for the first decade of their marriage, in over forty years, I have never heard them argue or raise their voices to each other. The only time I think it came close was when my mom learned, decades after the fact, that Dad went out with another girl the night before he asked Mom to marry him. He wanted to be absolutely sure that Mom was the right one. She was. Even though she never wanted to marry a farmer and prayed that she would marry a preacher or a teacher, she did indeed marry a farmer, but with her encouragement, he blossomed as both preacher and teacher. And she became the perfect preacher's wife.

The family grew to include six children, five of us born within nine years (I came at the end of that string) and a sixth born ten years later when my parents were in their forties. I've already mentioned that Dad did sometimes raise his voice to the six of us kids. I think that quite possibly I brought it out in him more than any of the others. Dad had high expectations for all of us, and when we didn't live up to them, he let us know that. I only remember one time that Dad paddled me. Most of the time, his disappointment was all the punishment that was needed. Still, he never approached me or any of my siblings with a critical spirit when he corrected us, and we never doubted that we were loved.

Time with Dad was a premium commodity while I was growing up. At least two nights a week, he stayed in the dorm at the college because he finished teaching late and started teaching very early. However, although it might seem unusual to those who know him primarily from his work at Cincinnati Bible College and Seminary, it wasn't his work there that I really saw as the focus of his life. When people asked me what my father did, I told them he was a preacher. He spent 35 years in preaching ministry, enjoying every aspect in spite of the difficulties. He preached at the Hamersville Church of Christ from before I was born until after I had gone to college. (The other congregations he served were Pandora Church of Christ, Columbia Church of Christ, his home church, and Saltair Church of Christ.) At the height of his ministry in Hamersville, the church ran over 200 in a town of 600. Nearly everyone in the county knew him and respected him. People who never came to church listed him as their minister when they went to the hospital. He served as a dean of a junior week at the local church camp so long that his former campers brought their children to his week. Since the Friskneys had children in the local school district for more than twenty years (including four valedictorians), it's not surprising that Dad was elected to a four-year term on the school board, including one year as president, during which an addition for the high school was built.

I have often said, somewhat humorously, that growing up as a preacher's son is the best preparation for ministry—and the best preventative. But growing up as Dad's son, I couldn't help but grow up loving the church. While Dad's contributions to the school are impressive, nothing compares with the vigor with which he approached his church duties. When he got home from school, he went calling. On Saturdays, he typed and printed the church bulletin then brought the copies home for our family to fold in front of the television that night. (He often compensated us by popping corn over the fire in the fireplace.) But Sundays were the really impressive days. He taught a large Sunday School class and preached a sermon each Sunday morning. On Sunday evenings, he often led the singing in addition to preaching again. In between, every Sunday afternoon, he visited the sick and shut-in from the church, and some Sundays, he led a worship service at the local nursing home. Then after the evening service, he composed, typed, and printed the church newsletter for the week.

His passion for the local church has translated itself to deep concern for the church worldwide. He began teaching a Bible class for Japanese people while he was in the army. For many years, he has served on the standing committee of the Lake James School of Missions. He taught for a summer at Springdale College in Birmingham, England. He helped lead a study tour through Italy, Northern Africa, and the Holy Land. In addition, he has provided help and encouragement through speaking/teaching visits in Japan and Australia. Currently, he serves as mission chairman at the Bethel Church of Christ and on three mission boards. His expertise has also reached beyond his location through his writing, including three commentaries, several lesson series, and many contributions to periodicals and research materials.

Of course, no essay about my dad would be complete without discussing his commitment to Cincinnati Bible College and Seminary. His schooling there started in the fall of 1948 (culminating in AB, MA, and BD degrees), and his teaching began in 1954. His first responsibilities were in Greek and English, but through the years, he taught dozens of different courses in several fields. While he is probably best remembered for Greek, student favorites included 1 Corinthians and Revelation. But his contributions haven't been limited to the classroom. He served as dean of men and academic dean in short-term roles. His writing ability led to his writing the first student handbook (1966), being involved heavily in the self-study and accreditation report, and proofreading several catalogs and other pieces. He has been head of several departments: English, Bible and Theology, and Bible. He was class sponsor for four different classes, worked with the yearbook staff for over twenty years, and planned and planted several campus beautification projects. For these different areas of work, he was honored with the Teacher of the Year Award (1990), the Outstanding Alumni Award (1996), and "a few" Golden Eagle Awards from the American Yearbook Company. Still, Dad's greatest reward has been in the lives that he has influenced through the classroom, through advising, and in one-on-one relationships. He finds great satisfaction in knowing that he has prepared leadership to take his place at the college and in various areas of ministry.

One of the fascinating things about Dad's ministry has been his ability to balance his contributions to the local church and the Bible college. He explains the connection of the two in this way: "The church has priority. It came first, and the gates of hell will not prevail against it! The church has to continue Paul's challenge to Timothy (2 Tim 2:2). One of the ways in which this is done is in the Bible college. There can be a mutual need and mutual ministry between the two as the church does its work."

Of course, the reason Dad has worked so well in both fields is the fact that his strongest commitment is to God and the central relationship in his life is with Christ. As a child, I watched my father in many situations. He handled nearly everything well, but I could tell when he was uncomfortable when others couldn't. When he is uncomfortable, he chooses his words more carefully, so they don't flow as smoothly. However, I have never heard him stumble over words when he is praying. In speaking to God, he is at his most comfortable.

That relationship with Christ continues to sustain him in all aspects of life. I can remember many things from his sermons through the years. Once he said, "Many people talk about the Christian life as if it were something that we just endure until heaven. But even if there were no heaven, I would want to live as a Christian. It's the best life there is." His faith also allows him to look with expectation into the future. He does expect to continue his writing, his teaching, and other aspects of his ministry (as well as his gardening). But his humility and his vision both lead him to look elsewhere when he looks into contributions to come: "I have enjoyed seeing the extension of myself in my family, my church, and my community. It has been very satisfying to see how important faith and subsequent standards in life values are reflected in my family and my students. I expect them to go beyond my experience and service."

CHAPTER 2

The Church: The House of God: A Sermon on Matthew 16:15–18; Ephesians 2:19–22; 1 Peter 2:1–12

JACK COTTRELL

We know what a church building is. It is a physical structure made of wood, bricks, stones, concrete, or some such material. It is the place where Christians meet for teaching, fellowship, breaking bread, and prayer. Almost every "local church" has one. There are literally thousands and thousands of them across the land.

In the Old Testament the people of Israel had just one physical structure that might be called a "church building." It was the *temple* built in Jerusalem (preceded by the portable tabernacle). We should not think, however, that Israel's temple was simply the forerunner of the multitude of church buildings that have served God's people in New Testament times.

The fact is that Israel's temple has nothing to do with church buildings as such. As is the case with most physical things related to Israel, its counterpart under the New Covenant is something altogether on the spiritual level. That spiritual counterpart is the church of Jesus Christ itself—the called-out people, not a physical building.

The church of Jesus Christ is indeed figuratively spoken of as a building, and that is how we will speak of it here. Jesus said he would *build* his church (Matt 16:18); Paul says the church is a "building, being fitted together" (Eph 2:21); Peter says we are "being built up as a spiritual house" (1 Pet 2:5). This spiritual house, the people of God, is no less than God's New Covenant temple. Ephesians 2:21 says this spiritual building is "growing into a holy temple in the Lord." Paul asks, "Do you not know that you"—you, plural; you, the church as a group—"are a temple of God?" (1 Cor 3:16).

Sometimes as Christians we wonder why we exist as a local congregation of Christ's church. Why did someone think it was necessary to plant a church in this neighborhood? What is it supposed to be doing here? What is its purpose, its reason for existence?

One way to answer such questions is to compare the church with its Old Testament type or counterpart, the temple. What was the role of the temple in the life of Israel? What purposes did it serve? When we answer these questions, we will also know the purposes of the spiritual house of God today.

The ideas we are presenting come mainly from 1 Peter 2:5: "You also, as living stones, are being built up as a spiritual house for a holy priesthood, to offer up spiritual sacrifices acceptable to God through Jesus Christ."

1. The Church Is a Refuge From Death

Even though the church is a *spiritual* house, Peter says it is made out of stones. Each "stone" is an individual person, with all the members of the church being built up together into one beautiful building.

Perhaps the most interesting thing about this is that Peter calls the material from which the church is built *living* stones. What does this mean? It means that those who become part of the church receive the gift of life. The very first purpose of the church is to be a refuge from death and a source of life.

1.1. Israel's Temple Was a Refuge from Death

Of course, we know that the primary purpose of the tabernacle and temple was something else. But these Old Testament structures did in fact serve as a place of refuge for a person being unjustly pursued by someone who wanted to murder him.

The Mosaic Law actually specified six cities other than Jerusalem as "cities of refuge," to which such a person could flee and be protected from revenge killing until it could be determined whether he really deserved it. The Old Testament indicates, though, that the people of Israel concluded that the temple could serve the same purpose. It records a couple of cases in which someone fearing for his life fled to the tabernacle and "took hold of the horns of the altar" (1 Kgs 1:49–59; 2:28–35). Nehemiah may be reflecting this practice when he says after being threatened, "Should a man like me flee? And could one such as I go into the temple to save his life? I will not go in" (Neh 6:11).

1.2. The Church Is a Refuge from Death

Whether the world realizes it or not, mankind's greatest enemy is death—death in all its forms. Every unrepentant and unconverted sinner is already in a state of *spiritual* death (Eph 2:1, 5). His soul is devoid of true sensitivity toward God and is filled with the decay of sin. *Physical* death likewise starts gripping its ugly fist around us as soon as we come into the world. We know it will crush us; we just don't know when. Most fearful of all is the *eternal* death in the lake of fire that awaits the sinner who is still a sinner when his body dies.

Many people ignore this enemy, or they think they have found ways to avoid its vicious and fatal blows. They are like the religious leaders in Old Testament Jerusalem in Isaiah's time, whom the prophet mockingly pictures as declaring, "We have made a covenant with death, and with Sheol [the place of death] we have made a pact. The overwhelming scourge will not reach us when it passes by, for we have made falsehood our refuge and we have concealed ourselves with deception" (Isa 28:15).

People today still create deceptive myths to convince themselves that they have death licked. Consider believers in reincarnation, for example, or those who visit spiritists. Consider the impact of the many reports of "near-death" experiences. Consider the desperation of those who have themselves frozen at the point of death, hoping to be revived someday. What Isaiah said to his contemporaries still applies: when the torrent of death bears down upon you, your refuge of lies will be swept away (28:17–19), like a tidal wave smashing a beach umbrella.

But Isaiah gave us this promise from God: "Behold, I am laying in Zion a stone, a tested stone, a costly cornerstone for the foundation, firmly placed. He who believes in it will not be disturbed" (Isa 28:16).

This is probably the passage to which Jesus is alluding when he says, "Upon this rock I will build my church; and the gates of Hades shall not overpower it" (Matt 16:18). Hades is the same as Sheol in Isaiah 28. It refers to the place of death, the forces of death, the power of death. Jesus is saying, "Let me build you into my church, on the solid rock foundation that God has laid for it in my death and resurrection, and you will find true freedom from the scourge of death. I will make you a *living stone*. You will overcome death in all its forms."

One of the first things that happens to a believer, a person who lets Christ build him into his church, is that the believer is raised from the dead. The gift of the Holy Spirit banishes that state of spiritual death, and the baptized believer becomes spiritually alive toward God. The believer has the promise that his body will be raised from the dead one day in a glorious form, and that he will *not* be cast into the lake of fire which is the second death.

That is, as long as the believer remains *in the church*. For it is the *church*, the spiritual house that Jesus is building, that is the only refuge from death. This is one of its main purposes. This is part of the gospel that Christians preach to the world: When you become a part of the body of Christ, you become a *living stone*. Death has no more power over you.

This is the first truth: this spiritual house called the church is the only sure refuge from death. But this text sets out another purpose for the church.

2. The Church Is God's Dwelling Place

Peter says these living stones are being used to build a "spiritual *house*." Now, the usual purpose for a house is to be somebody's dwelling place, the place where somebody lives. This is true of the church. It is God's house. He lives in it. Remember that we are not talking about a physical church building, although we sometimes call it "God's house." The real house of God is the people of God.

2.1. Israel's Temple Was the House of God

The Old Testament describes first the tabernacle and then the temple as "the house of the Lord" and "the house of God" (1 Chron 28:12). God himself called it "my house" (1 Chron 28:6). Jesus called it "my Father's house" (John 2:16). This was true not just in the sense that it *belonged* to him, but that he actually lived in it.

Well, not in an absolute sense, of course, as if he lived there and nowhere else. Even Solomon, who built the first temple at Jerusalem, understood this. He said, "But will God indeed dwell on the earth? Behold, heaven cannot contain thee, how much less this house which I have built!" (1 Kgs 8:27).

Nevertheless in some real way God did set his presence upon and within the temple. When the original tabernacle was completed, God's visible, cloud-like presence covered it and filled it (Exod 40:34–35). When its replacement, the Jerusalem temple, was dedicated, the same thing happened: "The cloud filled the house of the Lord" (1 Kgs 8:10). The people knew that the temple was holy (Ps 79:1), or separate and different from all other such places, because God's presence was there, especially in the innermost sanctum called "the holy of holies" or "the most holy place" (1 Kgs 8:6).

In what ways was God present in his house, his temple? First, the temple was a house for God's *name*. God called it "a house for my name" (1 Kgs 8:18). "My name shall be there," he declared (1 Kgs 8:29). God's "name" stands for all that he is: his sovereign power, his holy character, his gracious love. That the temple was associated with the name of God meant that it was a kind of symbol of the reality of God both for Israel and for the nations (see 1 Kgs 8:41–45). To defile or destroy the temple was to defile the very name of God and challenge his sovereignty.

Second, the temple was a house for God's *word*. As soon as the temple was built, Solomon ordered the leaders of Israel to place the ark of the covenant within it (2 Chron 5:2). "Then the priests brought the ark of the covenant of the Lord to its place, into the inner sanctuary of the house, to the holy of holies" (2 Chron 5:7). The only things in this ark or chest were the two stone tablets on which God had written his ten commandments (2 Chron 5:10).

Third, the temple was a house for God's *heart*. The Lord declared, "Now My eyes shall be open and My ears attentive to the prayer offered in this place. For now I have chosen and consecrated this house that My name may be there forever, and My eyes and My heart will be there perpetually" (2 Chron 7:15–16). Because the people of Israel knew the temple was God's dwelling place, they called the temple a house of prayer

(Matt 21:13). This is why God said that his eyes and ears and even his heart were there, indicating that he would hear his people's prayers and that his heart wanted to answer them.

Finally, it was a house for his *glory*. This especially refers to the cloud-like presence. "The glory of the Lord filled the tabernacle" when it was built (Exod 40:34–35), and the same happened to Solomon's temple (1 Kgs 8:11; 2 Chron 7:1–3). When the people of Israel realized that the temple was a house for the presence of God's glory, their natural response was worship: they "bowed down on the pavement with their faces to the ground and they worshiped and gave praise to the Lord" (2 Chron 7:3).

2.2. The Church Is the House of God Today

Peter says the church is a spiritual house, and Paul makes it clear that it is a house in which God dwells on the earth today. "You are being built together into a dwelling of God in the Spirit," he says (Eph 2:22). You, the church, are the temple of God, he says, and "the Spirit of God dwells in you" (1 Cor 3:16).

Each individual Christian's body is a temple for the Holy Spirit (1 Cor 6:19), but so is the church collectively, as a body. It is true that God is everywhere, and that not even the totality of created space can contain his presence. So in that sense God is present among Buddhists, Hindus, Moslems, and even atheists. But he does not *live* among them, so to speak. Only the church can be called his dwelling place. He lives among the people of the church in a special way. This is where he is welcome; this is where he "feels at home," or where it is natural for him to be.

The church is the house for his *name* today. He lives in the church; his name is on the church's mailbox, so to speak. Solomon said, "I am about to build a house for the name of the Lord my God" (2 Chron 2:4). Today Jesus is building a house for *his* name; he calls it "my church" (Matt 16:18). This is why churches proudly wear the name "church of Christ" or "Christian church." This is the inconsistency of churches calling themselves by other, denominational names. To do so is like a family putting someone else's name on their mailbox at home.

The church is the house for God's *word* today. Churches of the Restoration Movement want to be known as "the New Testament church." The Bible and the Bible alone is their only rule of faith and practice. They are a "people of the Book." Just as the temple housed the tablets of the ten commandments, so has God written his word on the very hearts of his New Covenant people (Heb 8:8–11). It is the church's responsibility to know and proclaim his word, and to live by it before the world. Like the first church at Jerusalem, the church must continually devote itself to "the apostles' teaching" (Acts 2:42).

The church is the house for God's *heart* today. It is the focus of his love: "Christ also loved the church and gave Himself up for her" (Eph 5:25). His heart is with the church, and he is on the side of the people of the church. He is near to the church, and he hears the prayers of the church. The first congregation devoted themselves to prayer (Acts 2:42), and so should today's church.

The church is the house for God's *glory*. In the midst of a world that has sunk to the lowest depths of falsehood and decadence, the church should be the one place where the glory of God shines forth. Other people should be able to look at the church and *see God* in the world. This is the tragedy of moral lapses among church leaders, and the tragedy of moral mediocrity within the church as a whole.

Recently I was driven past a newly built Mormon temple. I was told that the Mormon church chose the site very carefully. Their goal was to find the land that had the highest elevation in the area, so that the building would stand out for miles around. This is what God expects, not of church buildings, but of the church itself. The church should expect to be the visible evidence of the glory of God, as established by its lifestyle and its witness. As Jesus said, his followers are the salt of the earth and the light of the world. He expects them to shine the light of God's glory from the highest ground. "Let your light so shine before men in such a way that they may see your good works, and glorify your Father who is in heaven" (Matt 5:13–16).

3. The Church Is a Holy Priesthood

In 1 Peter 2:5 the apostle says that we as living stones are being built up as a spiritual house *for a holy priesthood*. Further on he refers to the church as a "royal priesthood" (v. 9). This means that every church member is a priest. The Protestant tradition has always spoken of the priesthood of all believers, in contrast with the Roman Catholic Church, in which only ordained clergymen can function as priests.

Now, what does it mean to be a priest? What do priests do? In what sense does the church function as a priesthood? Peter says that as priests we are meant to "offer up spiritual sacrifices."

3.1. Israel's Temple Was Where Priests Offered Sacrifices

Sacrifices and offerings played a large role in Old Testament worship and piety. The temple was the location where these sacrifices and offerings were made. Burnt offerings were sacrificed on the altar in the courtyard of the temple, and certain offerings of incense and bread were offered inside the temple itself. Blood from some of the animal sacrifices was offered within the temple, upon the mercy seat in the holy of holies.

One of the major functions of the Old Testament priesthood was to offer these sacrifices up to God on behalf of the people. For example, when an Israelite committed a certain sin, he had to sacrifice a guilt offering to God. In the case of a poor person this could be two young pigeons, one for a sin offering and one for a guilt offering. Here is how it was done:

> And he [the sinner] shall bring them to the priest, who shall offer first that which is for the sin offering and shall nip its head at the front of its neck, but he shall not sever it. He shall also sprinkle some of the blood of the sin offering on the side of the altar, while the rest of the blood shall be drained out at the base of the altar.

The priest then burned the second pigeon on the altar (Lev 5:7–10).

Another example is the animals sacrificed on the Day of Atonement. The high priest first killed a bull as a sin offering for himself, then a goat as a sin offering for the people. After each slaying, the high priest took some of the animal's blood into the temple and sprinkled it on and around the mercy seat in the holy of holies (Lev 16:11–15).

What was the purpose of these and other sacrifices? In almost every case the priest offered the sacrifices *on behalf of someone else*. Other people brought their sacrifices to the Lord, as a way of restoring or expressing their communion with him; but the priests offered the animals to God on their behalf. In doing so the priests were mediating between God and the people, bringing them into God's presence and making them acceptable to him. In this sense "the priest shall make atonement for them, and they shall be forgiven" (Lev 4:20).

This is the nature and purpose of the priesthood of Jesus Christ, our "great high priest" (Heb 4:14). He offered up to God the sacrifice of himself, in order to make atonement for sinners and make us acceptable in the presence of God.

3.2. The Church Offers Spiritual Sacrifices

The work of Old Testament priests is the background of Peter's remark that the church as God's spiritual house or temple today includes the functions of a holy priesthood. As with the old priesthood, our task and purpose are to bring other people to God.

We are speaking, of course, of *evangelism*, which in many ways is the main purpose of the church. This is why the church exists in a community: to win the people of the community to Jesus Christ. Evangelism is sometimes likened to a harvest, with the church "going forth and reaping" and "bringing in the sheaves" (see Ps 126:6). In the context of 1 Peter 2:5, we could change the song to "bringing in the stones." Christians are stone-gatherers. They go forth to collect dead stones (sinners) and lead them to Jesus, who turns them into living stones and builds them into his spiritual house.

How is this purpose carried out in terms of priesthood? We must remember that the main function of priests is to offer sacrifices. The Mosaic priests offered physical sacrifices such as goats and pigeons, but Peter says Christians offer up "spiritual sacrifices." What are these "spiritual sacrifices"? There are two kinds.

First are the sacrifices of *good words*, with which we bear witness to the power of God's grace, including the personal testimony of how we ourselves have been saved from our sins. In 1 Peter 2:9, where Peter calls the church a "royal priesthood," he says that God gave you that task so "that you may proclaim the excellencies of Him who has called you out of darkness into His marvelous light." This is the "sacrifice of praise to God, that is, the fruit of lips that give thanks to His name" (Heb 13:15).

The point of priesthood, though, is that Christians do not offer up these sacrifices in private, but rather in the presence of the world. Peter says to *proclaim* God's excellencies, or publish them abroad. The Christian priest is thus a trumpet, a newspaper. Without being obnoxious he is always testifying to others. He is always looking for an opportunity to say in some way, "We interrupt this regular daily routine in order to bring you the following announcement: Jesus saves!"

The second kind of sacrifices is *good works*. This includes living a life of holiness before the world. Christians are after all a *holy* priesthood. They need to be aware that their holy living is not just to please God but to attract others to him. To this end Peter says to "abstain from fleshly lusts," and "keep your behavior excellent among the Gentiles, so that…they may on account of your good deeds, as they observe them, glorify God in the day of visitation" (1 Pet 2:11–12).

The sacrifices of good works also include works of service and benevolence within the community as a whole. As Hebrews 13:16 says, "And do not neglect doing good and sharing; for with such sacrifices God is pleased." By helping someone in need, a Christian shows him the love of Christ and draws him to Christ. This is priestly work.

Community service activities by the church draw not only those who are directly helped thereby, but also those who observe what the church does. Here we come back to Jesus' exhortation to "let your light shine before men in such a way that they may see your good works, and glorify your Father in heaven" (Matt 5:16). The point of doing such good works is not to bring praise to ourselves, but to cause others to glorify God and thus to want to surrender to him. This is how acts of Christian love and service become *priestly* work, and serve the purpose of evangelism.

What sorts of activities can function as such priestly sacrifices? Many churches already do such things as distribute Thanksgiving or Christmas baskets, maintain a food pantry or clothing closet for the needy, and perform services for the elderly such as cleaning their gutters or raking their leaves. There are many possibilities. Christians could read to the blind, take them shopping, visit people in nursing homes, do hospital volunteer work—all in the name of Christ. I know of a congregation in which the ladies' group had a regular project of making cancer bandages for a local hospital. It became priestly work when they invited non-Christian ladies from the community to join them in this good work, and in the process witnessed to these ladies and won them to Christ.

What Christians need to do as priests is to use their imaginations, to be creative in devising ways to offer up the sacrifices of good works. They need to renounce the couch-potato lifestyle, to shake out the cobwebs and the moss of inactivity. Remember, a mossy church gathers no stones!

4. Conclusion

We have been discussing the purpose of the church. We have seen that the church is God's spiritual house today, serving purposes like those of the temple in the Old Testament times. It is a refuge from death; it is God's dwelling place; it is a holy priesthood whose sacrifices of good words and good works bring other people into the presence of God.

This leaves us to ask about our own particular "spiritual house," the local congregations to which we all belong. How well do we fulfill God's purposes for the church's existence?

CHAPTER 3

Eating and Drinking in the Kingdom of God: The Emmaus Episode and the Meal Motif in Luke-Acts

JON A. WEATHERLY

Carefully prepared, balanced meals, we are told, are good for the body and for the mind. Not only do nutritionists urge us to get the nourishment that comes from a variety of foods, social scientists remind us that we need the regular, interpersonal contact commonly experienced at a shared meal. Occasional snacks, eaten alone, simply do not offer the same benefit as the full dinner shared with family. Pursuing a common metaphor, we see that the same is true for our feeding on the Bread of Life. Is there a lesson that Tom Friskney has stressed more to his students than that the Scriptures must be read not in snack-sized bits but in dinner-sized chunks—with all of the context's courses served up—and not just for the benefit of the individual but for the blessing of the whole people of God?

What I present here is an attempt to serve up such a meal. The narrative of Jesus' appearance to the two disciples on the road to Emmaus (Luke 24:13–35) is a text that defies reduction to snack size. It is a fine example of Luke's literary artistry, a tightly composed, dramatic account that carries the reader from beginning to end without interruption, evoking sympathy, excitement and wonder. Included in it are provocative details that suggest connections to prior elements of Luke's Gospel and forthcoming details of his second volume, Acts. Blended together, these ingredients in Luke's literary and historical recipe focus the reader's attention on Jesus' climactic fulfillment of God's promises. Prominent in the recipe is the scene at the table. The Emmaus episode can be characterized as a centerpiece in Luke's portrayal of meals in his two volumes, meals that celebrate the fulfillment of God's promised salvation and express the shared identity of God's people as those who have received that salvation. As one who has been nourished countless times by Tom Friskney's exegesis—not to mention having been many times literally fed at his and Ruth's table and from his garden, I offer this interpretive repast to celebrate what he has done in the name of that salvation.

1. The Crafted Emphasis of the Emmaus Episode

This first story in Luke of an appearance of the resurrected Jesus brings together several themes that develop through the book and exemplifies a number of Luke's habits of writing. While these elements are accessible to all readers, they are most obvious to the reader of Luke's own Greek text. The story is a meal to be savored, with all the ingredients of the original recipe included.

Among those original elements is the introductory phrase, in current discussion commonly called a discourse marker, καὶ ἰδοῦ (*kai idou*, "and behold," v. 13). To many readers, such a phrase is a quaint part of the antiquated or holy style of biblical language. In part, this insight is correct, as Luke probably uses such expressions throughout his two volumes in imitation of the style of the Septuagint. But they provide more than stylistic flavor; these phrases also serve to draw the reader's attention to the action that immediately follows. At the beginning of the story, καὶ ἰδοῦ suggests that what ensues is of great importance and links the immediately preceding pericope, the crucial account of the women at the tomb, to a seemingly benign introduction of two disciples making an ordinary journey. It invites the reader to look for clues to the importance of this ordinary occurrence, suggesting that the real significance of the event may not be readily apparent at first. Already Luke is preparing for the unexpected revelation that will follow.

Similarly, Luke uses καὶ ἐγένετο (*kai egeneto*, "and it happened," vv. 15, 30) later in the narrative to draw attention to crucial turns of events. The first occurrence marks the entrance of Jesus, his identity hidden to the disciples. The second marks the corresponding revelation of Jesus' identity at the evening meal in the breaking of bread. This phrase, the common Septuagint translation of a Hebrew phrase that marks the beginning of a narrative or an important juncture within a narrative, serves to let the reader in on a secret still hidden from the characters. We the readers know the significance of Jesus' appearance while it is still hidden from the disciples.

English translations can only approximate the effect of Greek verb tenses. In this story, as elsewhere in Luke-Acts, the Greek imperfect tense is used to describe the setting of the main action. Actions like the journeying in v. 13, the discussion in v. 14, Jesus' journeying along with the disciples in v. 15, and even the crucial restraining of the disciples' eyes in v. 16 are related in the imperfect tense, emphasizing a continuing aspect to these actions. Thus the scene is set for the action related with a finite verb in the aorist tense, "he said," in v. 17. Jesus' words become the first focal point of the narrative and begin the discussion that will lead to the dramatic revelation.

Not that all the scene-setting material is superfluous, however: readers who have made their way through Luke's Gospel recognize a recurrent idea in v. 16. Time and again, Jesus' identity and teaching have been misunderstood, especially in connection with his death. The idea is most obvious in 9:45 and again in 18:34, where Jesus speaks directly of his impending death, but the disciples fail to understand. This ignorance on the disciples' part occurs repeatedly. Peter, who confesses Jesus as "the Messiah of God" in 9:20, utterly misses the significance of Jesus' transfiguration (and his death in Jerusalem, 9:31) in 9:33, "not knowing what he was saying." In the upper room, the disciples again display their ignorance as they argue over who is greatest (22:24–27) and misconstrue Jesus' remark about swords (22:35–38, 49–51). As with the passion predictions, this misunderstanding is centered in Jesus' submission to death in fulfillment of God's purpose. The disciples do not grasp that such is his mission, much less that Jesus' mission defines their own. But we cannot fault the disciples alone for such misunderstanding: in 2:49 Jesus' parents similarly cannot grasp the significance of his being about "my Father's things."[1] In the Emmaus story Luke makes the point of this motif clear. Jesus is definitively revealed only by God's initiative in his res-

[1] The singular pronoun "my" possessing "Father" in reference to God is exceptional in the discourse of first-century Judaism and is often cited as a subtle claim to a unique relationship between Jesus and God the Father (cf. Otto Hofius, "Father," in *New International Dictionary of New Testament Theology* [ed. Colin Brown; Grand Rapids: Zondervan, 1975–78] 1.618, 620).

urrection. Ignorance is the norm beforehand because the willing submission to death by one with divine authority is completely foreign to the outlook of all who surround Jesus. Jesus, as the promised Messiah sent by God to fulfill God's purpose, can only be truly understood as the one who gives his life in submission to God. And that truth can only be known as God vindicates his servant Jesus by raising him from the dead.

The ignorance of the disciples and the revelation in the resurrection of Jesus therefore becomes the object of pointed irony as the Emmaus story develops. The disciples' response to the still-hidden Jesus expresses shock at what they take as his ignorance. In contrast, the narrator shows that Jesus, marked with a Greek emphatic pronoun, is the only one who truly does know "the things that have happened in Jerusalem in these days" (v. 18). The disciples' explanation of these events mixes elements of truth with continued misunderstanding. Jesus was indeed a powerful prophet (v. 19), though he was much more. For the disciples, that power stands at odds with recent events (v. 20): the powerful one appears to have been overcome by others more powerful than himself. Jesus has been defeated by his enemies in the temple hierarchy. His followers, in contrast to the ostensible leaders of Israel (a contrast stressed by another Greek emphatic pronoun), had seen Jesus as the one who would actually redeem Israel, but after three days, such hopes are disappointed. Their only glimmer of renewed hope comes from the report of the women (v. 22), whose gender renders their witness questionable in this culture.[2] Their report of an empty tomb has been confirmed by the men (v. 24), but the disciples have no response to their account of angels who say that Jesus is alive. They are flummoxed, and their serious, animated conversation expresses their perplexity (vv. 15, 17).

This puzzle needs Jesus to solve it. Addressing the two disciples with language that recalls the description of the twelve in 9:45, he explains the death of the Messiah as a necessity in God's plan and as the

---

[2] The Gospels report that women were the first witnesses of the empty tomb runs against the cultural prejudice of the first century to distrust the testimony of women (cf. Josephus, *Antiquities* 4.8.15). This surprising element suggests strongly that the report is historical, not a creation of the later church. For Luke, the point in 24:22–23 is the irony that the culturally less credible witnesses prove to be reliable, as the "outsiders" often prove more faithful than "insiders."

prelude to the Messiah's glory. That glory can mean nothing less than the accomplishment of God's central saving purpose, the fulfilling of the promises expressed in all of Israel's Scriptures. Luke does not narrate Jesus' exposition of those Scriptures, but the reader of his two volumes would expect something like the biblical expositions in the speeches of Acts 2, 3, and 13. In other words, the promised Davidic king (Ps 16:8–11; Acts 2:25–28; 13:23) and Mosaic prophet (Deut 18:15–19; Acts 3:22–23), in whom God himself has entered history to redeem Israel (Ps 110:1; Luke 20:42–43; Acts 2:34–35), takes the role of suffering servant and righteous sufferer (Isa 52:13–53:12; Acts 3:26; 8:32–35), serving his followers and so accomplishing God's will. God has always acted on behalf of those who are weak and insignificant; now he has acted for them in one who has willingly assumed the most abject weakness. Israel's God has saved Israel by serving his servants (Luke 12:37; 22:27).[3]

As the prophetic word was the prelude to the event in Jesus' birth (Luke 1–2) and his death (Luke 9:22, 44; 18:31–33), and as the prophesied event must occur to make clear the meaning of the prophetic word, so it is here. Jesus' exposition makes the hearts of the disciples burn, but they realize as much only after he is revealed to them directly. The scene of vv. 28–29 portrays the common practice of hospitality in the Ancient Near East. The disciples, having arrived at what is apparently their home, are obliged to offer their fellow traveler a table and a bed; Jesus, the invited guest, politely refuses before accepting the customary accommodation. This much Luke's readers expect, but then Jesus the guest acts as host (v. 30) as he breaks the bread. This surprising gesture recalls Jesus' action in the upper room in 22:19.[4] We probably ask the wrong question

[3] A growing consensus among scholars of Luke-Acts is that the books portray the gospel of Jesus and the church founded upon it as the true restoration of Israel as promised by Israel's prophets. For a recent discussion see the various essays in David P. Moessner, ed., *Jesus and the Heritage of Israel: Luke's Narrative Claim upon Israel's Legacy* (Luke the Interpreter of Israel 1; Harrisburg, PA: Trinity Press International, 1999).

[4] Joel B. Green rightly criticizes those who see the Emmaus episode as a sort of enactment of the eucharist (*The Gospel of Luke* [New International Commentary on the New Testament; Grand Rapids: Eerdmans, 1997] 843). It is unlikely that gospel pericopae were composed or redacted to serve as symbolic references to church practices. However, it is not at all unlikely that church practices like the Lord's Supper were under-

if we wonder whether Luke portrays this meal as an observance of the Lord's Supper, but much suggests that Luke narrates the breaking of bread to show us the significance of the Last Supper and Lord's Supper. In the upper room Jesus' distribution of bread and cup to his disciples was introduced with his pledge not to partake of food and drink again until the coming of God's kingdom (22:16). Now, as he sits at a meal with two of his discouraged disciples, still during the Feast of Unleavened Bread that celebrates God's redemption of his people in the exodus and the wilderness, that pledge is fulfilled. As the guest joins in the festal meal as host, he is revealed as the risen Jesus, indeed the one who redeems Israel, whose resurrection inaugurates the promised kingdom of God. If we fear that we have exaggerated the significance of this gesture, we need only note v. 35: the breaking of bread is crucial in this decisive revelation of Jesus' identity.

Similarly, if we ask whether the disciples were unable to perceive Jesus because of divine, supernatural intervention or because of natural cognitive dissonance, we probably miss Luke's point. A cogent case can be made that the passive verbs ἐκρατοῦντο (*ekratounto*, "were restrained," v. 16) and διηνοίχθησαν (*diênoichthêsan*, "were opened," v. 31) are instances where the passive voice is used as a circumlocution for the action of God, the so-called "divine passive." However, the wider context indicates that Luke interprets the disciples' failure to understand Jesus and his mission as a clash between their deeply ingrained, value-laden expectations and the surprising plan of God and its outworking. But for Luke the natural versus supernatural conflict is not at all operative. The divine plan anticipates the misunderstanding and rejection that Jesus experiences; in fact, God's plan appears even to cultivate misunderstanding and rejection as prior to his death Jesus speaks cryptically and acts mysteriously. But it is the action of God, bringing to reality the plan of God, that also confronts and ultimately corrects that misunderstanding on the other side of Jesus' death. God expects and intends that his Messiah will be misunderstood and rejected, and God acts, by whatever specific means, to reveal his Messiah definitively. We need not

---

stood to be reminiscent of a series of meaningful actions in the ministry of Jesus and earlier in sacred history (cf. discussion below and Green, *Luke*, 851).

wonder whether the two on the road recognized Jesus when they saw the wounds on his wrists as he broke the bread or whether they knew him by direct, supernatural revelation, or whether some combination of the two was at work. As far as Luke is concerned, the disciples recognized Jesus because God acted deliberately to reveal him.

This revelation embraces more than just the identity of their insightful fellow traveler. It is the revelation that Jesus is genuinely raised from the dead, and that this resurrection is indeed the fulfillment of the prophetic Scriptures, the predictions of Jesus and the words of the angels at the tomb. It effects the redemption of Israel for which the disciples had hoped. With this event, they are able to perceive what they had misapprehended before: that God's work is accomplished through suffering in the service of his people, or, in words that Paul reports from another episode of revelation, Christ's power is made perfect in weakness (2 Cor 12:9).

The response of the two in v. 33 reflects this sudden sea-change in their understanding. Disregarding their own warnings about the lateness of the hour (v. 29; in the ancient world, travel after dark was very hazardous), they immediately return the considerable distance that they had traveled (this explains the reason for the seemingly gratuitous note about the distance between Emmaus and Jerusalem in v. 13), abandoning their hearth-and-home destination to report their experience to the twelve. Such excitement, motivating what would otherwise appear to be foolish actions, underlines the astounding event that they have witnessed. This is more than the "mere resuscitation of Jesus' corpse," as some in our time caricature the bodily resurrection of Jesus. It is an event—necessarily in space and time, for God is redeeming his people who live in space and time—that reshapes their understanding of what God is doing in the world. The age of fulfillment, the restoration of God's reign, has begun in this dramatic and unexpected resurrection of Jesus.

In this story Luke blends carefully chosen words, deliberately crafted sentences and dramatic narrative development to make his point. But the point stands out most clearly when we hear another element of his literary craft, the echoes of other scenes in the rest of his account and of Israel's sacred Scriptures, with which Luke and his readers were intimately familiar.[5] We turn now to consider one category of these, the meal or feast.

2. Feasting in Luke's Gospel

Jesus' action at the table of Emmaus is all the more striking because it comes at the end of a series of meals that he shares with his followers.[6] In keeping with the synoptic tradition, Luke stresses that Jesus ate meals with "sinners."[7] The die is cast in 5:29–32, where Jesus answers the Pharisees' objection to his feasting with sinners with a statement implying that his eating with them is a crucial part of God's program to reclaim his sinful people for himself, "I have not come to call the righteous but sinners to repentance" (5:32). The significance of this episode for understanding Jesus' ministry has recently been stressed by E. P. Sanders. He has argued that the controversy surrounding Jesus' association with "sinners" is not coherent in the text of the gospels as it stands. The idea of restoring sinners by means of repentance was not controversial among the Pharisees or other first-century Jews, who were all very much in favor of the idea of repentance. Sanders' solution is to hypothesize

---

[5]That Luke was a Gentile (a likely inference from Col 4:11, 14) is popularly taken as a basis for the conclusion that he and his readers were relatively less concerned for Jewish matters like the fulfillment of the Scriptures. The actual content of Luke-Acts, replete as it is with quotations of an allusions to the Scriptures, indicates otherwise. Luke may have been a Gentile, and he certainly wrote for people outside the geographical boundaries of Israel. But he was steeped in the scriptures, traditions and worldview of Judaism.

[6] For additional perspectives on the meal motif in Luke's Gospel, see David P. Moessner, *Lord of the Banquet: The Literary and Theological Significance of the Lukan Travel Narrative* (Minneapolis: Fortress, 1989).

[7] By "synoptic tradition" I refer to the oral teaching, apostolic in origin, which circulated in the first generation of Christianity and served as the basis for the synoptic gospels (cf. Luke 1:2). With a significant minority of scholars, I see this oral material, rather than direct literary dependence among the synoptics, as the most plausible explanation for the similarities and differences among the synoptics, the so-called synoptic problem (cf. Bo Ivar Reicke, *The Roots of the Synoptic Gospels* [Philadelphia: Fortress, 1986]; Kenneth E. Bailey, "Middle Eastern Oral Tradition and the Synoptic Gospels," *Expository Times* 106 [1995] 363–36; N. T. Wright, *Jesus and the Victory of God* [Minneapolis: Fortress, 1996] 133–37).

against the text that Jesus associated with sinners apart from repentance.[8] To this issue N. T. Wright has brought a penetrating proposal: that what was controversial about Jesus' action was not that he omitted repentance but that he mediated forgiveness to the repentant sinner directly, on his own authority and by means of association with his own person. Jesus, in effect, claimed to displace the temple as the mediator of forgiveness and reconciliation.[9]

Later meals with sinners in Luke's Gospel continue to drive home this idea. In 7:37–50 Jesus' feet are washed and anointed by a sinful woman, whose action he explains as the expression of profound gratitude for the forgiveness that she has received (7:47). Jesus takes for granted that such gratitude should be expressed directly to him and pronounces directly at the end of the pericope that the woman's sins are forgiven (7:48) and that her faith, by her actions obviously directed to Jesus, has saved her (7:50). She has rightly honored the source of her forgiveness at the table, while the host, who denies that Jesus possesses any such authority (7:39, 49), neglects even the most basic gestures of hospitality (7:45–46) because he does not know the gratitude of the one who has genuinely been forgiven. Here the table is the place where those who recognize Jesus as God's agent of salvation celebrate what they have received through him. And so "wisdom" is indeed "vindicated by her children" (7:35) as those who object to Jesus' feasting with sinners (7:34) have their foil in those sinners who join in the celebration.

This is no less the case than in Jesus' extended rejoinder to the Pharisees' objection in Luke 15. The three lost-and-found parables end on the note of celebration (15:6, 9, 22–24, 32) that mirrors the celebration in the presence of God (15:7, 10). Jesus mediates the celebrated forgiveness himself, directly, without recourse to the temple. It prompts rejoicing in heaven because it fulfills the reconciling and restoring purpose of the gracious God depicted in the father of the third parable. Not to join in the celebration is therefore to stand at odds with God's purpose in the world.

---

8 E. P. Sanders, *Jesus and Judaism* (Philadelphia: Fortress, 1985) 174–211.

9 Wright, *Victory*, 264–74.

These meals with sinners have a close counterpart in Jesus' feeding of the five thousand (9:10–17). The wilderness setting of this story (9:12) does more than explain the need for the provision of food; it ties the miracle to the miracle of manna in the wilderness. The account portrays Jesus as the prophet like Moses, who leads Israel out of a greater bondage than Egypt to a greater promise than the land. Significantly, in Luke this story immediately precedes Peter's confession of Jesus and its crucial aftermath, climaxing in the transfiguration that reveals Jesus' identity to the faltering disciples as Jesus discusses his own ἔξοδος (*exodos*, "departure" or "exodus," v. 31) with Moses and Elijah. The wilderness meal, like the mountaintop christophany, reveals who Jesus is and what he does. Between the two is the confession of that identity and the revelation of the mission: the Christ of God will die in Jerusalem.

I have already drawn attention to the connection between the Emmaus meal and the Lukan Last Supper. Here it should be added that Luke's account of a distribution of cup (22:17), bread (22:19) and cup again (22:20) ties the representation of Jesus' body and blood even more closely to the Passover (cf. 22:15). Though some have suggested that Luke's account expressed some variation in early Christian observance of the Lord's Supper that involved two sharings of the cup, the more obvious explanation is that the first cup is the last in Jesus' observance of the Passover. This connection to Passover recalls the wilderness feeding and now explicitly identifies Jesus' death as the fulfillment of God's promise. Jesus dies for his followers (22:19) to effect a new covenant (22:20). Here is the means by which Jesus has welcomed sinners into fellowship with God without the mediation of the temple: his own death is explained in sacrificial terms; it mediates the "new" covenant by which God restores his relationship with his people after the exile (Jer 31:31–34). His death is therefore to be remembered by this meal (22:19) as the Passover meal remembers the exodus, for it accomplishes God's promised salvation.

Taken together, these meal-scenes suggest a deliberate compositional emphasis on Luke's part, what is often termed a motif, a recurring narrative element that draws together various parts of the story and articulates a cumulative idea. In Luke's Gospel, meals with Jesus are occasions in which the salvation of God is revealed and celebrated. The breaking of bread in Emmaus brings that motif to its climax, at the end of a purposeful series of such meals.

3. The Shared Meal in Acts

If this understanding represents Luke's point, we should expect to see the revelation and celebration continue in Acts. And such is the case. Meals are not especially frequent in Acts, but references to them come at crucial points in the story.

The most obvious of these is the double reference to the breaking of bread in Acts 2:42, 46. Discussion of these references generally has focused on whether either or both refer to observance of the Lord's Supper. This question is important, and it can perhaps be settled better when we observe the significance of the meal motif in Luke's Gospel. There the meal shared with Jesus repeatedly signifies the celebration of God's mighty act of redemption even before it is explicitly connected to the symbols of body and blood. In Acts 2:42–47, Luke portrays the Jerusalem church in terms that suggest the fulfillment of God's ideal for his people. Unlike their counterparts in the wilderness with Moses, and unlike the belligerent, bickering, wavering disciples in Luke's Gospel, the followers of Jesus are now marked by their generous, harmonious life together and their habitual devotion to God. They are the people of the last days, constituted as such because through his death, resurrection and ascension Jesus has been exalted to the place of divine authority from which he gives the promise of the last days, the Holy Spirit. The common meals express and celebrate this new state of affairs. The believers eat together to rejoice together because of what God has done and, in fulfillment of God's purpose for his people, to care for one another's needs (cf. 4:32–37; Deut 15:4). Both aspects of these meals are grounded in the redemptive death of Jesus by which he served his followers; thus, a specific commemoration of Jesus' death is utterly congruent with Luke's portrayal. Elsewhere in the New Testament we see that Christians commonly observed the commemorative Lord's Supper in the context of a larger shared meal (1 Cor 11:17–34). For Luke the distinction between shared meal and Lord's Supper is probably unimportant, and Christian practice may have been to commemorate Jesus' death in the shared bread and cup at every meal that Christians observed together. In this important summary statement near the beginning of Acts, Luke gives a programmatic statement about the community of Jesus' followers. As God's people in the age of fulfillment, they eat together, expressing the common life they enjoy through the death and resurrection of Jesus.

What makes this portrayal all the more significant is the implicit comparison with Israel's practices under the Mosaic Law. Three great feasts—Passover, Weeks (Pentecost), and Tabernacles—marked the Mosaic calendar. To these were added Purim, celebrating the deliverance through Esther from Haman, and Hanukkah, celebrating deliverance through Judas Maccabaeus from Antiochus Epiphanes. All explicitly celebrated the actions of God to redeem his people and provide for them. Luke shows a similar practice of feasts celebrating God's saving actions. These, however, are not annual feasts but weekly or even daily ones. Such an extravagant practice fits a people who know themselves to have received the zenith of God's blessing.

This comparison is all the more likely to be deliberate in light of Isaiah's picture of God's great act of salvation in terms of a great feast (Isa 25:6–9). Following God's judgment on all the nations (Isa 13–24), he promises to fulfill his saving intention for all the nations, not just Israel, on "this mountain," that is Mt. Zion or Jerusalem. Luke's portrayal suggests echoes of this prophetic image. The early church in that very place observes its celebration of salvation accomplished, but the celebration will ultimately embrace all the earth.

Later in Acts the celebratory meal makes brief but provocative appearances. Saul in Damascus fasts until his baptism; only then does he eat (Acts 9:9, 19). Peter's offense in the conversion of Cornelius is his eating with Gentiles (11:3), offensive not just because it threatened ceremonial impurity but because it represented a welcoming of the uncircumcised into the celebration of God's salvation received. Peter's response demonstrates that God is now fulfilling his promise to prepare the banquet of salvation for "all peoples" (Isa 25:6). Similarly, the neglect of the Greek-speaking widows in the distribution of food is probably more than a "practical" matter alone, as the shared food represented inclusion in the community of God's people (6:1). In Troas the church meets with Paul for the explicit purpose of breaking bread (20:7); notably, the meal itself begins after Paul has restored Eutychus to life (20:11), his deliverance, like all the miracles of Acts, serving as a token of the larger salvation of God at work in Jesus and his people.

The end of this series comes in Acts 27:34–36, where Paul breaks bread and distributes it to all on the storm-ravaged ship. Luke presents this meal as first of all a practical matter: having gone for fourteen days without food, they need to be strengthened for the rigors ahead (27:33–34). But the matter does not stop with this. Paul tells his shipmates that the food is for their σωτηρία (*sôtêria*, "preservation" or "salvation," v. 34). Certainly he does not imply that by merely eating the bread, they will be "saved" in the theological sense. But in the account of Paul's deliverance from shipwreck, Luke conveys a point that he makes in other accounts of divine intervention that brings tangible protection or restoration. Paul's preservation, along with all others on the ship, is a concrete token that points to the larger, comprehensive salvation that Paul has received in Jesus. This salvation is at work regardless of outward, visible circumstances, but sometimes it is dramatically manifested in the visible sphere. So, as Jesus the guest acted as host in Emmaus, now Paul the prisoner acts has host in breaking the bread (27:35). The action expresses his own confidence, as one who belongs to the sovereign God through Jesus, that God will indeed deliver him and his companions from the impending shipwreck, just as God has promised. Paul is going to Rome, despite the plight of his outward circumstances, in fulfillment of the will of God and through the power of God. While it is unlikely that Luke wants the reader to see this action as an observance of the Lord's Supper per se, it is very likely that he wants the reader to see the same celebration and revelation in this breaking of bread as in the more explicitly eucharistic settings. In this action Paul is confidently declaring that God will deliver this company. This act of salvation points to the larger salvation of which Paul is a beneficiary and a chosen emissary. In this action Paul is therefore also revealed as such, a revelation confirmed as his predictions are fulfilled and as he continues his progress to Rome, where he preaches "boldly and unhindered" (28:28).

In short, the church of Acts follows Jesus' own practice of celebrating God's salvation in a shared meal. As Jesus' meals revealed or declared his identity as God's agent of salvation and celebrated the reception of that salvation, so the meals of Acts reveal or declare the church of Jesus to be the people of God in the age of fulfillment and celebrate with joy and confidence the salvation that that identity entails.

4. Continuing the Celebration: Observations on Current Practices

What does all this say to the church in our time and place? Potentially, it says much, but I will focus on a few implications that flow out of the two aspects, revelation and celebration, that have been observed above.

In a culture like nineteenth-century America where Christian ideas and the story of Jesus were widely known, one perhaps could take for granted that the revelatory aspects of the Lord's Supper were easily received. Churches could observe the Lord's Supper and reasonably expect that most outsiders visiting their services would be familiar enough with the significance of the act to understand it. In our now very different culture, such may no longer be the case. For that reason, "seeker sensitive" worship dictates for many that the Lord's Supper not be observed except in services in which "seekers" are not present. Such concern is understandable if the Lord's Supper is viewed as an obscure religious observance with meaning only for the initiated. However, Luke's portrayal of the revelation of Jesus' identity and mission in the shared meal could suggest a different perspective. The meal, accompanied by the words that explain it (Luke 22:19–20 and parallels) may well continue to be a most appropriate means of declaring the Lord's death (1 Cor 11:26), even for those who have not heard before.

This impact will likely be all the more powerful if the celebratory aspect of the shared meal is rightly considered. Most American observance of the Lord's Supper is infused with silence, introspection and sorrow. While such may be fitting for one aspect of what we remember, the Lord's death for sin, Luke's portrayal of overflowing joy, fellowship and confidence in trial suggests that our observance lacks some critical elements. Were the joy of salvation in the resurrected Jesus as palpable in the Lord's Supper as it is in a lively song service, then unbelievers and believers both might have a better sense of what the gospel is really all about. Are there means by which such joy can be shared among Christians at the table today? I suspect that those who know that joy can think of many ways to express it together when they share the bread and cup. Likewise, though the travails of life sometimes mean that believers observe the feast alone, such solitary observance does not fully realize the shared experience at the center of the act.

Discussion of the Lord's Supper has traditionally centered on its meaning (transubstantiation versus consubstantiation versus symbolic memorial) or frequency (weekly versus less than weekly). Recently the introduction of worship services on days other than Sunday has prompted debate over the appropriateness of observance on other days. The discussion here suggests that these controversies are certainly not in view with Luke's meal motif; nevertheless, the implication of Luke's narration may tend to ameliorate some of the debate. Recognizing the wide range of events and texts evoked by the shared festive meal tends to set aside the notion of "presence" in the elements. The point is that God's action in Jesus' death is celebrated in the larger context of God's actions and promises, a theme far from assertions about nuances of presence. Who would think to assert some sort of mystical presence of Christ in the elements when the focus is on remembering the climax of a series of saving events? As to frequency, the very range and richness of associations in the shared meal argue strongly for its frequent observance, quite apart from questions of precedent. Can the person who understands the fulfillment of God's promise in Jesus be satisfied with merely occasional celebration of it? At the same time, can such celebration be limited to just one day of the week? Though a cogent argument can be made for the commemorative value of observing the Lord's Supper among the Lord's people on the Lord's Day, the day of Jesus' resurrection, such does not forbid other times of joyous observance. Indeed, the reader of Luke and Acts is struck by the extravagant frequency with which Jesus and his church feast together to celebrate what God has done, not the limits placed on such celebration.

In all these considerations, however, we are looking at more than just the right way to "do church." We look instead to the tangible expression of joy and wonder shared by those who recognize that God has done what he promised in a most surprising way. Here is the real outcome of Luke's narrative. Restoring such a sense to our hearts—and not just in partaking of the bread and loaf—is likewise a real part of restoring the

Christianity of which Luke was a part. For Christians like Luke, life is a banquet.

CHAPTER 4

Conflict in Acts: A Faithful Reading

JAMES A. SMITH

Professor Friskney's approach to Scripture is indelibly inscribed into everything I teach and write about the Bible. Specifically, I cite his famous course on Revelation as a moment of revelation in my own life when for the first time the text became alive in a way previously foreign to me. What I have to offer in this celebration of Professor Friskney's life and work is a summary of some earlier work in which I attempt to read Acts in terms of the principles I gleaned from the many courses I took under his instruction.

In the tradition of the Restoration movement, the book of Acts finds itself in a rather privileged position. The trend is to read Acts as if it were a collection of unchanging rules with a keen eye cast upon the text in search of "apostolic precedence," thereby creating the tendency to make Acts alone the last word on what is appropriate or normative for how we "do church." While Acts is without doubt a valuable resource for our contemporary church, it is the case that the tradition of the Restoration Movement has privileged just one of the book's many features, sometimes even to the exclusion of its other features. This exclusion is somewhat problematic when given the evangelical reverence for the Bible as the final source of authority. This present essay is a reading of the narrative which allows Luke to achieve some goals which have been largely pushed aside by traditional readings.

In spite of the fact that it is a delightfully well-crafted, dynamic work deliberately written in narrative form, it is surprising that Acts is *rarely read as a narrative.*[1] It seems to be the case that when we allow

---

[1] Note the phrase "compile an account" (NASB) in Luke 1:1, based on the Greek ἀνατάξασθαι διήγησιν (*anataxasthai diêgêsin*). The standard English rendering of this

the narrative features of Acts to rise to the surface of our readings, we discover a more nuanced Acts capable of providing the reader, and the church in general, with far more than procedural notes on church polity. It is of course the case that the appreciation of narrative features within the New Testament texts, especially the Gospels, is hardly new information. It is unfortunate, however, that while theoretical appreciation of the New Testament narratives has been developing for some time, little attention has been paid to the way in which such readings actually do something for us, and impact the way in which these texts enable us to live out the Christian life. In a small way, I seek to redress that problem in this essay.

A comprehensive investigation into the Acts narrative or even one of its themes is clearly impossible in such an essay as this; however, I hope to present a brief overview of one aspect of the Acts narrative which I believe gives some insight into what can be achieved through careful attention to the narrative itself. Residing within the narrative of Acts there is a dynamic force that is latently apocalyptic (God's people ultimately win in spite of crisis), which Luke uses to provide strength for the victory of Christ's church, then and now. The particular narrative structure around which this dynamic force finds coherence is *conflict*.[2]

---

text fails to communicate all that Luke is suggesting in the Greek. A better translation would be "arrange a narrative." The word διήγησις (*diêgêsis*) is not a problematic word at all; it simply means "narrative" or "account" (Walter Bauer, Frederick Danker, W. F. Arndt, and F. W. Gingrich, *A Greek English Lexicon of the New Testament and Other Early Christian Literature* [3rd ed.; Chicago: University of Chicago Press, 2000] 245). However, when English readers see "account" they typically do not think "narrative." For this reason it is perhaps appropriate for us to employ the word "narrative" here in order to allow readers to appreciate that this is indeed what Luke has arranged for us. As to the relationship of the prologue in Luke to Acts, see Loveday Alexander, *The Preface to Luke's Gospel: Literary Convention and Social Context in Luke 1.1–4 and Acts 1.1* (Society for New Testament Studies Monograph Series 78; New York: Cambridge University Press, 1993).

[2] There have been many other attempts to develop conflict in the Gospel narratives, but virtually nothing in Acts. Malina and Neyrey briefly delve into the Acts narrative and use a social model of labeling and deviance theory to understand the dynamics of conflict within the forensic episodes of Acts (Bruce J. Malina and Jerome H. Neyrey, "Conflict in Luke-Acts: Labeling and Deviance Theory," in *The Social World of Luke-Acts* [ed. Jerome H. Neyrey; Peabody, Massachusetts: Hendrickson, 1991] 97–122). See also

1. The Basics of Reading Narratives

Before I go on, it is important to state some basic features of narratives pertinent to our discussion. All narratives are written from a particular perspective; thus, they represent the interests of the person composing the narrative. One of the most important things to keep in mind when reading a narrative about history, is that we are not reading the historical events themselves, but we are reading *about* the historical events. In the case of Acts, we are not reading the actual events of the early church; we are reading Luke's perspective on those events. The fact is, Luke could not present to us an "objective" account of the early Church even if he wanted to; he would always be relegated to offering his own perspective on the early church. The simple reason for this is that Luke cannot tell us *everything* that happened. He must de-select information from his narrative at the same time he selects information to be included in his narrative. This process whereby Luke decides what to put in and what to leave out is the process whereby he writes into the narrative his own perspective on those events. This is, of course, nothing new. We frequently speak of the theology of Matthew versus the theology of Mark when we discuss the Gospels. Such a discussion implies that both Matthew and Mark have different interests and thus offer us different perspectives on the story of Christ.

Another feature of narratives is the fact that they are made up of what are typically referred to as a "story" and a "discourse." The story of the narrative is the actual historical course of events lying behind the narrative. The discourse is the way in which that historical course of events is *represented* and laid out in the narrative. In other words, the story is the "what" and the discourse is the "how." When we come to experience narratives, which we have already noted are the results of a selection process, we find that along with the selection process comes an arrange-

---

James Smith, *Conflict in Acts: The Rhetoric of Power* (MA Thesis, Cincinnati Bible Seminary, 1995). With respect to the Gospels, Jack Kingsbury, whose literary analyses are somewhat weak and obvious, has been particularly active in this area; see Jack Kingsbury, "The Developing Conflict between Jesus and the Jewish Authorities in Matthew's Gospel: A Literary Critical Study," *Catholic Biblical Quarterly* 49 (1987) 57–73; *Conflict in Mark* (Minneapolis: Fortress, 1989); *Conflict in Luke* (Minneapolis: Fortress, 1991).

ment process. We are all quite used to this feature of narratives; thus none of us is terribly surprised if, when watching a movie, we see a "flash-back" (analepsis) to something that happened in the life of a character long before the story of the movie ever began. The appearance of a flashback in the narrative reflects the fact that there is a difference between the actual substance of the "story" and the way the story is arranged (the discourse). The same phenomenon is located throughout the synoptic Gospels as well; only on a few occasions do the synoptics arrange the selected events in the same order.

The fact that narratives are "arranged" is one of their more highly significant features and has been recognized as such since Aristotle wrote his *Poetics*. The arrangement process is employed by Luke with great success throughout the narrative to provide tension and drama, as well as to highlight important features of the story he is trying to relate. A particularly interesting feature of arrangement (which was also recognized by Aristotle well before Luke's time) is the sequencing or juxtaposing of two events so as to create a causal relationship between them. Take for example the following sentence: "While Tom was mowing the grass beside the house, he heard a crash and turned to see that a rock had gone through the window." The human mind naturally attempts to apply a structure to that sentence as we make the assumption that the rock probably came from Tom's lawnmower; thus the relationship between Tom's mowing and the smashed window is understood to be a causal one. Note, however, that the sentence does not require this scenario at all, but it does *suggest* this scenario through the dynamics of juxtaposition and sequence. Rather than argumentative syllogism, Luke uses juxtaposition to allow the reader to generate theological truth as a dynamic activity of the text working upon the reader.

Reading Acts therefore needs to be a process whereby we take stock of what Luke is doing in the discourse of the narrative, and how he is using the discursive features of the narrative to achieve his goals. We recognize that there is always a story behind the discourse, the historical events being represented by that arrangement, yet we also recognize that our access to those historical events is always preceded by Luke's selection and arrangement process. In the end, we are always reading *Luke* and we should never fail to keep this in mind as we read.

2. Conflict, Power, and the Program of Acts

Conflict in Acts serves as more than a mere literary device with which to propel the narrative forward.[3] Luke is doing much more than just telling us about what happened in the past; he rather uses the narrative to project an experience of the world that works to either reinforce or subvert the reader's worldview. As with all narratives, the very nature of Acts is to invite the reader to enter into and experience the world of its story, but in so doing it either critiques points of difference between the narrated world, and the world of the reader, or it will reinforce points of similarity between those two worlds. While Luke is doing a number of different things with the Acts narrative, the one which has the interest of this essay is the way he uses occasions of conflict to elucidate systems of power which are operating within the world.

Power is the ability to exert one's will upon another. It is the ability to make someone do or think something that they would otherwise not do or think.[4] A "power structure" is a system of power to which people subscribe (examples from Acts would be the religio-political structure of Jerusalem-centered Judaism, the pervasive political structure of the Ro-

[3] Conflict is a common means for moving narratives forward. An excellent example is the narrative found in J. R. Tolkien's *The Hobbit*. The protagonists need to achieve a particular goal. They start their quest as a rather naïve, disjointed group and through conflict they gain strength, skill, wisdom and unity which are the very things that enable them to ultimately achieve the object of their quest. In other words, conflict, rather than a hindrance, ironically became the means to move them forward in their quest. Good triumphs evil in spite of evil's attempt to waylay or stop it from progressing.

[4] Note for example the oldest extant novel, the Greek classic *Callirhoe* by Chariton (G.P. Goold, ed. and trans., *Callirhoe* by Chariton, [Loeb Classical Library 481; Cambridge, Mass.: Harvard University Press, 1995]). The story is about a person named Callirhoe who travels under the auspices of the goddess Aphrodite. The significance of the relationship between *Callirhoe* and Acts is that the journey motif signifies the power of the deity to bring about the deity's goals through the human agent regardless of the circumstances the agent encounters. In the mid-twentieth century, Henry Cadbury noted that he did "not know where one can get so many illustrations of the idiom and ideas of the author of Acts in 150 pages as in the love story (*Callirhoe*) of [Luke's] near contemporary, Chariton of Aphrodisias" (Henry J. Cadbury, *The Book of Acts in History* [New York: Harper and Brothers, 1955], 8). See also Douglas R. Edwards, "Acts of the Apostles and the Greco-Roman World: Narrative Communication in Social Contexts," *Society of Biblical Literature Seminar Papers* (1989) 372, n. 51.

man Empire, pagan religious beliefs, nature, and so forth). All of us subordinate ourselves to one system of power or another. Through occasions of conflict, Luke is able to bring to light what kind of power structures exist in his world and highlight their interaction as each contends for the dominant position. In Luke's narrative, the Christian Way proves to be the dominant and true source of power operating in the world; whereas other power structures are shown to be subordinate to the power structure to which the early church subscribed.

Luke uses conflict in Acts to highlight the fact that there is a deity who has an agenda that is being worked out among humans by other humans. When this plan is hindered by other power structures, the power structure according to which the Christians operate *overcomes* the opposing power structure. In so doing, Luke presents the power structure of those who serve this deity as superior to all others, thereby challenging the worldview of the reader who assumed the dominance of a different power structure. Luke presents conflict in such a way so as to perform a rhetorical function which challenges the reader to accept his point of view. That is, Luke's narrative presents a challenge to the reader by presenting an historical story about a God operating powerfully in this world. The result is either to effect a sense of hope and confidence in God upon the Christian reader of Acts or to present something of an evangelistic challenge to non-Christian readers by showing them the dominance of the Christian God, the source of true power.

If we consider for a moment the basic structural makeup of Acts, we can lay down a framework which will help us to appreciate what Luke is trying to achieve in the design of his narrative. The discourse essentially begins with a re-telling of the ascension scene from Luke's Gospel. We note that Luke has already changed the way he told the event in his Gospel.[5] The last thing Jesus mentions in the Gospel is the coming of the Holy Spirit; in Acts the last thing that Jesus says is perhaps the most important comment in the entire narrative: "you shall be my witnesses both in Jerusalem and in all Judea and Samaria, and even to the remotest part of the earth" (Acts 1:8). The focus has now turned from the story of Je-

[5] Note that the texts in Luke 24:46–49 and Acts 1:7–8 evidence both selection and arrangement differences.

sus' life and teaching to the spread and development of the gospel; thus, we find that Jesus' comment functions as the "program" for how the Acts narrative unfolds.

There's more to the program of Acts, however, than its geographical dimension, which is typically the main point made about Acts 1:8. More important than the geographic arrangement is the fact that the message of Jesus Christ goes out under the auspices of the Holy Spirit's power and moves through hostile territory; thus, the program immediately sets up a preliminary, but fundamental conflict: the spreading of the gospel is commissioned and the ultimate goal is the "ends of the earth." That is, the program of Acts, and ultimately for the church in general, is about taking the gospel into what Paul characterizes in Colossians as the "domain of darkness."

Conflict is thus fundamental to the Christian mission, since evangelism is a process that engages itself in the oldest conflict in both history and pre-history: the conflict between God and his opponents. Reading conflict in Acts is therefore not a mere literary task; it is a deeply theological activity attempting to elucidate what is fundamental to the Christian mission. The fact is that we tend to miss its significance in Acts because we fail to connect the way Luke is using historical events to highlight the operation and interaction of power structures within the world. When we read Luke's use of conflict in Acts, we see that the skirmishes between the Christians and their various opponents are representative of a more fundamental struggle and that Luke is trying to say something much bigger than simply what happened in the first few years of the church's life.

The larger structure of Acts bears out the basic point Luke is trying to make. The program stated in 1:8 is the movement and spread of the gospel from Jerusalem to the "ends of the earth," which, as mentioned, reflects a fundamental, primordial conflict between God and his opponents. If we skip forward to the end of the discourse to see how things turned out, we find the Apostle Paul, the new champion of the faith, in Rome (the political and cultural center of the known world), preaching the gospel unhindered.[6] That is, the structure of Acts itself bears out fea-

[6] Note the grammar of Acts 28:3–31: Paul is receiving any who would come to him, and that reception is characterised by his *on-going* preaching and teaching. There is

tures of Luke's theology which represent his understanding of the nature of the gospel and its proclamation. Acts uses conflict to reflect God's greater activity in the world, and the cumulative effect of an entire narrative full of conflict is to say something about how God realizes his activity in the lives of ordinary people. Thus, when we compare the program in 1:8 to Paul's activity in Rome, which is, as far as the narrative is concerned, the realization of the program, then we see that Luke is suggesting that the Christian faith is representative of God's on-going activity in human history.

3. The Rhetoric of Conflict in Acts

It is apparent from the narrative's basic structure that the overarching movement of the narrative is the spread and development of the gospel. What we need to ask now is "What significance does that movement bear for our contemporary reading and application of Acts-as-a-whole?" If we take the movement of the gospel as primary in the development of the narrative, how does that contextualize the "meaning" of Acts? This is where conflict comes in. Conflict, as it is being used here, is the dynamic that arises when the gospel attempts to move forward and encounters an obstacle to that movement. Ironically, what we observe in the narrative is that obstacles representative of opposing power structures operating

---

the inevitable question here as to whether the phrase "ends of the earth" is a reference to Rome. It is generally understood that by the time Paul gets to Rome, Christianity has already arrived. Yet, as far as the narrative goes, the phrase is equal to Rome. Rome has been characterized in a similar way before this by the likes of Lucian. The important point here is that *functionally* speaking the great proclaimer of the gospel, the Apostle Paul, has arrived in a place to which all roads lead and from which all roads go. Once the *proclamation* of the gospel is in Rome, it is everywhere; thus Rome is at least representative of the "ends of the earth" because Rome is connected to the rest of the world. Hemer notes that the gospel's arrival in Rome and not Paul's is indeed the real climax of the narrative, even though the climax is built around Paul. Colin J. Hemer, *The Book of Acts in the Setting of Hellenistic History* (ed. Conrad Gempf; Winona Lake, IN: Eisenbrauns, 1990) 383. Barrett states the obvious here: "The truth probably is that the phrase does refer to Rome, but to Rome not as an end in itself but as representative of the whole world" (C. K. Barrett, *The Acts of the Apostles*, *The International Critical Commentary* [Edinburgh: T&T Clark, 1994] 1.80).

within the world never actually function as genuine hindrances; they rather always result in assisting the spread of the gospel. There is a rhetorical consequence to this fact which I hope to bring to the surface in the following re-tellings of conflict in Acts.

3.1. Peter and John in Conflict: 3:1–4:31

The first conflict to consider is in the Peter and John episode in Acts 3–4. Peter heals a lame man and catches the attention of those milling about the temple precincts. This gives Peter and John occasion to proclaim the gospel which subsequently draws the attention of the temple guards who proceed to throw them in jail. Thus begins the "proclamation-persecution" motif that drives the narrative to a climactic scene when Paul eventually enters Rome in Acts 28.

The immediate effects of the arrest in chapter 4 are also important. In 4:5–12 (especially vv. 10–12) the Jewish leaders are officially notified of the new power operating in the world. This of course sets into motion the specific series of conflicts which inadvertently pushes the proclamation of the gospel well beyond the bounds of the temple for the first time. The Jewish leaders, who represent an institutionalized system of power, are perplexed. They recognize that some power has been exercised but are unable to evaluate it in terms of how they assume power works, so they attempt to subdue it by virtue of those means to which their own understanding of power is accustomed: physical (this-world) force.[7] Peter and John are healing people and the leaders of Jerusalem are beating people.

Already the rhetorical effect is in place: the Christians begin to represent a power structure which has its source outside human activity, but both the source and expression of the Jewish leaders' power are entirely confined to this physical world. So, if we stopped the narrative at this point and asked the reader who has the real power, the inevitable answer is Peter and John, who have already pointed out that the power is not

[7] Acts 4:16–17 suggests that the leaders recognize that two kinds of power had been exerted: (1) supernatural: a well-known lame man has been healed (2) social: many people believed it happened and subscribed to the new power operating in the world (see 4:4).

theirs at all but God's (3:12–13). The jailing and the beating send Peter and John back to the Christian community with a realization of what is going to have to happen if this program (1:8) is to be fulfilled. They pray together (4:24–30) and recite occasions of conflict against Jesus and align the present persecution of the faith with the persecution of Jesus, thereby aligning themselves with God's purposes in the world.

Note that they really only pray for one thing: boldness of speech and the subsequent validation of that which is spoken (4:29–30); that is, they pray that they might be able to fulfill the program of spreading the gospel. The result of the prayer is that God ratifies the petition by shaking the building and enabling them all to speak "boldly." In other words, God is shown to have taken note of the persecution and will indeed grant the church the ability to proclaim the message of Christ in spite of persecution. This prayer serves as a proleptic portrait of what to expect as the narrative unfolds, namely that God himself stands behind the proclamation of the gospel; all who oppose the proclamation of the gospel oppose God.[8] What the reader must now do is to observe what happens when people who subscribe to structures of power in the world other than that of the gospel attempt to prevent the proclamation. This leads to an obser-

[8] This is the second recorded prayer of the nascent church. The first is the prayer offered before drawing lots for the apostle to take Judas' place in 1:24–25. The Acts 4 prayer, however, is the first in which the church's prayer concerns their mission in this world. It is therefore an important prayer, both in the narrative and historically. For the narrative, the prayer is proleptic as discussed above. Historically, the prayer demonstrates that the real interest of the apostolic church is proclamation, but not just any kind of proclamation—pointlessly bellowing out the words of the gospel message is not equal to the kind of proclamation envisaged here. The proclamation prayed for was to be done with "bold speech." The Greek word here, παρρησία (*parrêsia*), is a fairly significant term in the ancient world. It was often a reference to the particular kind of discourse used by a philosopher who fearlessly stated the truth before a tyrant. During the first century, the term was more typically used as a reference to the discourse of two kinds of people: someone who was a true friend telling the truth and avoiding flattery for the sake of the friend's betterment, and of a philosopher (no longer in the face of a tyrant) who did not use philosophy merely to please people and thus make a living (note for example Paul's comment in 1 Thess 2:5). "Bold speech" was a socially-charged concept which referred not to the form of the communication, rather to the willingness of the speaker to communicate without pretext. The same term is more commonly translated in non-biblical texts as "frank speech."

vation about the genius of Acts: it works in different ways for different readers but always towards the same basic end.

We also note that they do not pray for protection from persecution, nor anything at all for themselves; rather they pray for what is singularly paramount for the early church leaders, the ability to fulfill the program (1:8) through *proclamation of the gospel.* If there is one thing that the practice and strategy of the contemporary church needs to adopt from Acts, it is the subordination of everything else to the effective proclamation and spread of the gospel. With respect to that, we further note that as the narrative develops Luke recites the activities and practices of the apostles, but the idea that we ourselves should then mimic those very practices is a misguided one, since it displaces function for form. When reading Acts, our question must really be, "In what way did a particular 'act' of an apostle help the early church spread the gospel and thus promote the program?" That is, what we need to imitate is *why* the apostles did what they did, and not necessarily the formal actions themselves. Thus to answer the question of *why*, the answer invariably comes back: they did it to spread the gospel. If there is an apostolic precedent in Acts it is *expedience* for the sake of the gospel's spread and development.

Getting back to our narrative, we observe that if God stands behind the proclamation of the gospel, and the Jewish leaders oppose the proclamation, then clearly Luke is claiming that the Jewish leaders are opposing God. This of course invokes the subsequent well-known (but a little overdue) caveat offered by Gamaliel in 5:38–39 which takes place during the next attack upon the church (5:17–40). This attack is a response to the healthy growth of the church which is a direct result of the proclamation of the gospel. It is important to note that Luke draws our attention to the "jealousy" of the Jewish leaders as that which precipitates the attack. The thing which prompts this jealousy is the Jewish leaders' perception that there is a genuine threat to the stability of their own power structure. That is, more and more people are no longer subscribing to Jerusalem and its leadership as the center of real power in the world (or theologically speaking, as representative of God's will), but are rather acknowledging that Jesus Christ is the locus of real power and the so-called "Way" is the new means by which that power is realized in the lives of real people.

The Jewish leaders demonstrate that their power is really bound to this world when they employ physical power to hinder the spread of the gospel by throwing the apostles in jail. The "earth-boundness" of the Jewish leaders' power is highlighted by the fact that the apostles are no sooner in jail than they are set free by an angel of the Lord. The impotence and inferiority of the Jewish leaders is again highlighted in 5:21 when, blissfully unaware of the fact that the apostles had already been freed, they send for the prisoners to be brought before them. Their surprise is not only the discovery that their prisoners are gone, but also the discovery of the inadequacy of their own system of power—they cannot even keep these fellows in jail for the night, let alone stop their divine mission to spread the gospel.

3.2. Stephen in Conflict 6:7–8:3

The next significant conflict included by Luke is the martyrdom of Stephen in Acts 6:7–8:3. As an act of expedience, Stephen is chosen along with six other fellows to provide assistance that will enable the apostles to continue the program. We see that in 6:6 Luke alerts us to the potential for conflict with the Jerusalem power structure when he notes the degree to which the gospel has been spreading, even among the religious leaders. Stephen is challenged by some Jews who find they cannot cope with "the wisdom and the Spirit with which he was speaking" (which should cast the reader's mind back to the prayer in Acts 4). These Jews conspire to frame Stephen, and succeed in having him brought to trial. Stephen delivers a speech which recites a history of God interacting with his people, in order to point out the ironic history the Jews have of persecuting those who speak on behalf of God.[9] This of course resonates with the fact that the reader has already been made privy to other events in the narrative in which the Jewish leaders have failed to recognize God's activity. Stephen condemns the Jewish leaders, and they fail to control themselves and stone him to death.

Stephen is not just an ordinary character in the narrative, and Luke takes pains to demonstrate his extra-ordinary qualities: he is full of faith and the Holy Spirit (6:5), having wisdom (6:10), having the countenance

[9] Again, the motif of proclamation is a source of conflict.

of an angel (6:15), and he is enabled to see the glory of God, and Jesus standing beside God in heaven (7:56). Stephen is thus depicted as being entirely confluent with the purposes of God, yet the Jewish leaders ironically inflict upon Stephen the same thing that Stephen's speech had just pointed out was typical of Jewish treatment of God's spokesmen. Stephen is a spiritual man operating for God, and the Jewish leaders feel their power threatened and have him stoned. They try to stop with physical means what God is accomplishing through spiritual means.

The most important aspect of this event, however, is what happens next: systematic persecution of the church (8:1–3). Again, the attempt to stop physically what God is accomplishing spiritually fails miserably, and instead of stopping the advancement of the gospel, the persecution forces the gospel to spread: "a great persecution arose against the church *in Jerusalem* and they were all scattered through the regions of *Judea and Samaria*.... Therefore those who had been scattered went about preaching the word." The persecution of the church actually moves the narrative through perhaps its most significant development, namely, the spreading of the gospel beyond the confines of Jerusalem. Luke here indicates that the second stage of the program (1:8) has been reached; although we discover only later in the narrative that the *third* stage of the program was also initiated by this persecution. That is, in 11:19–21, Luke tells us that some of the people who were scattered by Stephen's persecution went to Phoenicia, Cyprus, and Antioch "speaking the word to no one except to Jews alone." However, some of these people, those from Cyprus and Cyrene, went into Antioch and also (11:20) proclaimed the gospel to *Greeks*! Thus the conflict arising after Stephen's martyrdom practically fulfills the entire program by itself. Proclamation led to persecution which inadvertently promoted the proclamation. Thus, again, conflict fails to hinder the gospel and rather inadvertently promotes the program of spreading the gospel to the ends of the earth. The God of the Christians has proved to be more powerful than all opponents thus far.

3.3. Paul in Conflict 18:5–17; 23:10–33

There is a large number of conflict episodes in Acts from which we could draw numerous examples. However, we shall limit the survey to just a few more examples. Two very interesting occasions of conflict in the narrative both involve Paul experiencing a vision from the Lord. They are interesting from the narrative arrangement perspective, since they rely heavily on the juxtaposing of narrative units to generate the desired rhetorical effect. We are going to observe each episode before commenting on them.

The first is Acts 18 where Paul is in Corinth. He has had the usual squabble with the synagogue and even succeeded in winning over the synagogue leader, Crispus. Naturally, this puts Paul and his gospel at strained odds with the Jews in the area. Paul's mission in Corinth seems to have been going very well after that (18:8), when suddenly the Lord appears to him in a vision. The content of the vision is interesting and once more harks back to the proclamation-persecution motif, and the confirmation seen in Acts 4 that the power of God stands behind the proclamation of the gospel. The Lord tells Paul not to be afraid but to "go on speaking and do not be silent, for I am with you and no one will attack you in order to harm you." Luke gives us a short summary that all was well during the rest of Paul's ministry at Corinth and then immediately moves on to recite a conflict episode which occurred during that time in 18:12–17.

In this episode, the reader moves from an exhortation by the Lord for Paul to continue speaking and his promise of protection, to an occasion in which Paul's ability to continue speaking and his general well-being are both threatened. The juxtaposing of these narrative units gives the reader an occasion to generate a causal link between them. By the time the reader reads 18:12–13 the question is raised: "what will become of Paul…will God be able to protect him and enable the gospel to continue?" Paul is brought up on charges; the Jews state their case to the Roman proconsul, Gallio; Paul goes to offer his own defense; he opens his mouth…and Gallio stops the proceedings. Suddenly the case against Paul is brought to a halt without Paul saying a word. Gallio was clearly uninterested in their problems and "drove them away from the judgment seat" (18:16). The result was that instead of Paul being attacked, the embarrassed Jews suddenly turned on their new leader and attacked him *on the floor in front of the judgment seat*! If the failure to bring charges against Paul, and the subsequent spectacle of a small mob of Jews beating their own leader on the floor of the court was not enough to embarrass the Jews, the final humiliation came when Gallio feigned disinterest in the brawl going on in front of him. In a culture which trades on honor and shame, the Jews have sustained a powerful blow to their social status, and Paul's gospel has sustained a significant social victory, which is of course extremely beneficial for the fulfillment of the program in Corinth.

The second Pauline episode is in Acts 23. Paul has been roughly put upon by the Jews in the temple and then subsequently rescued and arrested by the commander of the Roman cohort (Acts 21:27ff). The commander sets up an inquiry the next day where Paul has to confront the chief priests and the council. Paul causes a rift between the Pharisees and the Sadducees and Paul once again needs to be rescued by the Romans and kept in the barracks for the night. During the night, however, the Lord appears to Paul and tells him that he is to take courage because just as he has proclaimed the gospel at Jerusalem, he must also do so in Rome. In other words, we have a divine commission that Paul must go to Rome.

The very next thing the reader reads is about a plot by some Jews who had taken an oath to slay Paul before taking another bite of food. Will Paul be slain or will he go to Rome? Or perhaps, will God work his way in Paul, or will he be undone by the zealous Jews? The scheme looks well-supported, since there are forty participants in the oath and they had even sought approval and cooperation from the chief priests and elders; thus, the full-force of the Jerusalem power-structure is shown to be behind the scheme. It all sounds rather dark for Paul, that is of course until a small thread in the plot's weave appears to be left dangling. A young man hears of the plot. Unfortunately for the conspirators, the young man happened to be Paul's nephew, and he is quick to inform Paul of the scheme. Paul sends him off to the commander of the cohort, who circumvents the machinations of not just the forty men, but the entire Jerusalem power structure by sending Paul off to Caesarea. Aware that there are forty Jews out there plotting to kill Paul, the commander does not simply send Paul off with a couple of soldiers; he sends him off with two hundred soldiers, seventy horsemen, two hundred spearmen, and horses for Paul to ride—four hundred and seventy soldiers guard a mounted Paul against forty hungry Jews.

The plot is indeed foiled. Paul gets to Caesarea, spends some time there, and then when the Jews seem to have the upper hand in a trial before Festus, Paul invokes his citizenship and cries, "I appeal to Caesar!" thereby securing his passage to Rome, thus also demonstrating that God will have his way regardless of the machinations and opposition of human power.[10]

Both of these events highlight Luke's creative use of the narrative's discourse to create a rhetorical effect that has practical, theological implications. Interestingly, it is actually a rather contemporary maneuver reminiscent of post-modern communication; that is Luke, rather than stating the thesis, enables the reader to experience the thesis. The thesis, of course, is that which Professor Friskney has so well articulated throughout his teaching life: the New Testament has as a dominant theme, often lying in the effect of the text rather than as the linguistic sum of the text, that God is ultimately victorious and thus all those who work for God will also ultimately be victorious; the converse is a part of the same story: all who oppose God will ultimately be defeated.[11]

To be specific, in both episodes, Luke places an announcement from the Lord for Paul to take courage, clearly in the face of impending tribulation *of which Paul is unaware* (18:9; 23:11). Immediately following the announcements, there arises an occasion of specific antagonism towards Paul. In arranging the narrative thus, Luke is able to articulate for the reader the lines of the struggle for power between God's people and those who oppose God's purposes. For example, in the latter episode, God wants Paul to go to Rome; the Jews want to kill Paul before he goes anywhere. God and the Jews are once again shown to be at odds; thus the defining feature of the Jews here is not their race as much as it is their

[10] We recognize that Paul's Roman citizenship is debated. While we want to affirm that Luke is indeed writing with an agenda, the burden of the proof concerning Paul's citizenship is of course weighed upon an attempt to counter the rather significant weight of the demonstrably accurate history behind the narrative.

[11] Professor Friskney's reading of the New Testament suggested, before it was popular, that the New Testament as a whole constructs its dynamic qualities along the lines of a well-sustained apocalyptic movement. One of the points I hope to elucidate here is how that apocalyptic movement works itself out in Acts and subsequently in the contemporary church.

opposition to God's activity in the world. These Jews stand in the place of anyone who would oppose God and not at all for the Jewish people as a whole. The somewhat grandiose nature of Paul's departure from Jerusalem in Acts 23 is significant insofar as it demonstrates that God not only delivers Paul, but that he delivers Paul with great ease. Paul's later arrival in Rome (28:16), after having endured the storms, the deadly threat of Roman guards protecting their interests, the shipwreck, and the snakebite by a deadly snake, continues to demonstrate to the reader that the announcement in 23:11 is demonstrative of God's overarching and unsurpassed power within the world and in the face of both direct and oblique conflict.

By constructing the narrative in this way, Luke establishes causal links between God's will and the success of the program to spread the gospel in a world which is generally hostile to God's interests. By leaving the point unstated in the narrative, Luke enables the reader to experience the concept vicariously through the world of the narrative. This is the great power of narratives; they enable us to experience propositions. This is particularly significant of biblical narratives; they have a "theology," to be sure, but the propositional truth of that theology is found within the narrative's inner dynamic. For this reason, the theology we derive from Acts cannot be one that is based on (simplistic) surface-level or so-called "face value" observations of the linguistic sum of the text, because this is not at all the intended function of the narrative. In such cases, the narrative is like a circus animal being forced to perform tricks for us that it was never created to perform. The theology of Acts, or its applicability to our contemporary churches, can only be acquired through appreciation for the text-as-narrative, since Acts is in fact a narrative. Failure to account for Luke's creative selection and arrangement is simply a failure to seek what the author was trying to do and thus devalue the text by putting our own interests above it.

4. Conclusion: A Theology of Conflict in Acts

As mentioned above, there are many other occasions of conflict within the narrative that we could isolate and observe if space permitted. However, I would suggest that in so doing we would find the same point being made. By way of summary, therefore, let us briefly take stock of what Luke teaches us through observing his use of conflict in the narrative.

The entire narrative is predicated upon a divine commission to spread the gospel from Jerusalem to Judea and Samaria to the ends of the earth. When we then turn to the end of Acts, we find that the program has been for all practical purposes fulfilled; that is, we find Paul in Rome, at the very political center of the known world, openly preaching the gospel *without hindrance* (28:30–31). In this alone, we are able to observe something of the narrative's dynamic theology.[12] It also reminds us that if there is an apostolic precedent in Acts at all, it is that the proclamation of the gospel is to be paramount in the life of the church and that the "life" of the church is precisely the proclamation of the gospel.

The occasions of conflict within the narrative assist Luke in his goal of demonstrating the validity of the gospel message and the indomitable power of God it represents. The degree to which Luke is successful in demonstrating this validity and power is the degree to which Luke is able to present a narrative which offers both strength for Christian victory and an evangelistic challenge to accept the message proclaimed by the church. The evangelistic challenge derives from Luke's demonstration of the inferiority of Jerusalem, Rome, nature, magic, pagan religion, physical force, and even death when compared to the overarching power of the God of the Christians. The narrative is therefore similar to the confrontational force of parables; it requires a decision from the reader: accept what Luke is saying or reject it. The reader who accepts what Luke is saying then is required to accept the validity of the gospel and the superiority of the divine power behind it.

Perhaps one of the most poignant aspects of Professor Friskney's classes was the way he articulated the New Testament's relationship between faithfulness and hope. Hope helps us to realize in the present what we know to be true about the future. Hope in the New Testament is of course not simply wishful thinking; it is rather a fully convinced ex-

[12] That is, we see that Luke uses the narrative structure to show the readership two things: (1) this Jesus who commissioned the program in 1:8 has true power and cannot be ignored, either spiritually or politically; (2) the gospel message of Jesus must also be true. Insofar as the narrative does this, it shows itself to have evangelistic purposes to demonstrate the validity of the gospel of Jesus.

pectation. Our hope is that mechanism which enables us to remain faithful in the face of challenges to that very faithfulness. Luke's use of conflict in Acts establishes the Christian message as one which is backed up and validated by a victorious God. All who read Acts are able to derive hope for their present lives by observing God's historical activity in the life of the early church. Thus Acts provides "strength for victory" in the daily life of God's people.[13] Again, Acts achieves this by generating a sense of hope in the reader by showing actual situations in which God's power in the lives of real Christians was actively and aggressively challenged by significant opponents (in terms of this world) and yet remained victorious. The utter indomitability of that power in the life of the early church naturally provides encouragement for any contemporary Christian to be able to face conflict in his or her own life. All we need to do with Acts is to demonstrate that the God of Acts who went from victory to victory in the lives of the first Christians is the very same God served by contemporary Christians; thus contemporary Christians can have the same sense of hope and thus victory in their own lives as is demonstrated in the Acts narrative.

---

[13] *Strength for Victory* is the title of Professor Friskney's commentary on Revelation.

CHAPTER 5

The Deacon in the Pauline Church

TOM THATCHER

The term "deacon" is notoriously nondescript in the modern church. While many denominations recognize such an office, the functions of the "deacon" vary widely. Some "deacons" are primarily assistants to professional clergy in the work of teaching and sacraments; some are persons preparing for professional ministry who have not completed the requirements for full ordination; some have spiritual and administrative authority equal or superior to that of professional clergy; some are the executors of the congregation's legal and financial responsibilities. Aside from this confusion of roles, different standards are applied to determine which persons are suitable to serve as "deacons." In some cases candidates for this position must satisfy a particular code of virtues, often based on biblical passages such as 1 Timothy 3. Some are elected "deacons" because they possess professional or technical skills essential to the life of the congregation. Many churches install people in this position in hopes of increasing their involvement in the life of the congregation or their personal spiritual development; in these cases the primary "qualification" for installation is simply one's presence on the perimeter of the congregation. Widespread debate exists over whether gender is a qualification for the diaconate: must "deacons" be male, or can women hold this position as well? Specific ethical issues are also debated: does divorce, for example, disqualify a person from this position, or can persons whose children have left the faith serve as "deacons"? This confusion over duties and qualifications often discourages potential candidates and certainly does not assist "deacons" in fulfilling their responsibilities.

These difficulties are complicated by the fact that the New Testament has very little to say about deacons in the primitive church. A succinct list of stereotypical virtues which deacons should exhibit is offered in 1 Timothy 3, but this passage is strangely silent on the actual duties of such people in the Pauline churches. The title itself offers little assistance. The Greek word for this role, διάκονος (*diakonos*), was a generic term in the ancient world for a servant or assistant.[1] Paul rarely uses the term, preferring to refer to such persons as δοῦλοι (*douloi*), "slaves." It is clear, however, that διάκονος was used as a title in the Pauline churches for persons of a specific status. Deacons appear alongside overseers/elders, a fixture of Pauline congregations in Acts (14:23; 20:17), at Philippians 1:1, distinguishing them from "all the saints" in that city. Deacons also appear with overseers in 1 Timothy 3. But while it is evident that such a position existed in the Pauline churches, the Pauline letters always seem to assume that the reader knows who these people are and what they do. Little specific information is offered.

While the διάκονος is rare in the Pauline letters, the related term διακονία (*diakonia*), "service" or "aid," is somewhat more frequent.[2] This word is generally used in reference to specific types or acts of Christian service. This essay will first explore the Pauline concept of "service," διακονία, in search of clues to the specific role of the "deacon/servant," διάκονος, in the Pauline churches. Such an investigation will provide a framework for the "qualifications" for this position outlined in 1 Timothy 3.

1. "Ministry" (Διακονία) in Pauline Thought

In the Pauline letters, "service"/διακονία is integrally related to giftedness, to the utilization of powers or talents given to the individual by God. It will therefore be necessary to explore the relationship between gifts, the use of gifts, and the gifted person in Pauline thought.

While modern conceptions of spiritual gifts often begin with, or focus on, miraculous powers, Paul's concept of spiritual gifts begins with

---

[1]See Walter Bauer, Frederick W. Danker, William F. Arndt and F. Wilbur Gingrich, *A Greek-English Lexicon of the New Testament and Other Early Christian Literature* (3rd ed.; Chicago: University of Chicago Press, 2000) 230–31.

[2]See Bauer, Danker, Arndt, Gingrich, *Lexicon*, 230.

the relationship between God, individuals, and the congregation. This perspective is particularly evident in Ephesians 4:7–13. Here the "gifts" which the ascended Christ has bestowed upon the church are not abstract powers but individuals, stereotyped according to the positions they fulfill. "Apostles," "prophets," "evangelists," "shepherds/pastors" and "teachers" are all "gifts" given to prepare believers "for the work of service" (εἰς ἔργων διακονίας [*eis ergôn diakonias*], 4:12). The degree to which persons and abstract powers can merge as "gifts" in Paul's thinking is most evident in 1 Corinthians 12:27–30. Paul there lists people whom God has "appointed" in the church, all found in Ephesians 4: apostles, prophets, and teachers. In this case, however, Paul continues the list with a number of abstract powers which God has given to individuals within the church: miracles, healing, helping, administration, and tongues. Lest the reader think that such abstract gifts operate apart from the individuals who use them, Paul personalizes this second list in a series of rhetorical questions at 12:29–30. There are miracles, but not all are miracle workers; there are healings, but not all are healers; there are tongues, but not all are tongues-speakers. In Paul's view, "gifts" are active and valuable to the church only as they proceed from God and operate through specific individuals. For this reason, a "gift" is not an abstract power or office but a person who uses such power or fulfills such office.

A number of gifts in the list at 1 Corinthians 12:29–30 are obviously "miraculous," in the sense that they involve the exhibition of supernatural powers beyond human ability. Paul therefore refers to such gifts as "manifestations of the Spirit" (12:7), offering special wisdom and knowledge, healing, works of power, prophecy, tongues and interpretation as examples (12:8–10). While the modern reader is tempted to distinguish such gifts from those of the "teacher" or "evangelist" at Ephesians 4:11, it is important to note that Paul does not make such a distinction. Hence, at Romans 12:6–8 Paul also lists as God-given "gifts" more "natural" abilities such as "service" (διακονία), teaching, exhortation, charitable benevolence, leadership, and compassion. While "gifts" of this sort may not "manifest the Spirit" quite so directly as others, Paul insists that they, too, are God's gift of grace (12:6) to be used humbly for the good of the entire group. In short, Paul views any talent which might be useful to the Christian community as a gracious gift from God which must be utilized in service to the church.

It is Paul's understanding of specific abilities within a "grace" framework which allows him to speak of both natural and supernatural abilities as "gifts." Paul understands Christian conversion within a death/resurrection paradigm. The believer no longer lives; rather, Christ lives and operates in the world through the recreated believer (Gal 2:19–20; Rom 6:1–11). The bestowal of this resurrection life is an act of grace on God's part (Eph 2:1–10). Consequently, Paul thinks of any abilities possessed by the Christian, natural or supernatural in origin, as "gifts" of God given to serve the church. For example, the Christian healer, having died in conversion, has received the supernatural power to heal in the present resurrection life. Obviously, this power represents a new element in the experience of the gifted person. At the same time, however, the person possessed of strong leadership skills, perhaps acquired through life experience or leadership training, dies in conversion and, in Paul's view, receives back from God this leadership ability as a gracious gift in the resurrection life. While leadership ability may not represent a new element in the experience of this person, its recontextualization within a Christian life in the Christian community makes it a "gift," an operation of God through the individual directed toward the needs of the church. In both cases the individual believer is viewed as a conduit for this divine activity, an administrator of a divine tool for the sake of the Body. This perspective allows Paul to conclude that every Christian has received a gracious "gift" with which to serve the church (Eph 4:7), whether natural or supernatural in origin.

This approach to Christian "service"/διακονία, the individual acting as a conduit for divine action, informs Paul's own self-image as a servant of God and the gospel. At Ephesians 3:7 Paul refers to himself as a διάκονος (KJV and NASB = "minister"; NIV = "servant") of the "mystery of Christ," which he understands to be the proclamation of salvation to Gentiles (3:4–6). His role as διάκονος is clarified at 3:9 in reference to God's "administration" of this mystery in salvation history. "Administration" here is the Greek word οἰκονομία (*oikonomia*), "stewardship," a term which Paul has already used at 3:2 to discuss his reception of the "stewardship" of God's grace toward the Gentiles. Paul uses similar terminology to describe his own role at 1 Corinthians 4:1, where he refers to himself as an οἰκονόμος (*oikonomos*), "steward," of the mystery concerning Gentile salvation. The "steward" in the ancient world was a domestic slave who managed the master's household goods and funds, similar to the modern accountant. "Stewardship" is the process of managing another person's accounts in this fashion. Paul is a "steward" of the mystery in the sense that the gospel proceeds from, and belongs to, God, while he himself simply manages or administers this property. This is apparently the sense in which Paul understands his role as διάκονος/"servant" at Ephesians 3:7: he is the vessel through which God's grace flows out into the Gentile world.

This same understanding of διακονία, "service," is evident in Acts 6:1–6, the choosing of the Seven.[3] While the term διάκονος/deacon does not appear in this context, διακονία and the verb διακονέω (*diakoneô*) are both present. At 6:3 the Twelve inform the assembly that they cannot neglect their duties of spiritual leadership "in order to serve (διακονεῖν [*diakonein*]) tables." "Serving tables" here refers to the distribution of benevolent funds, the transfer of money via a third party who simply acts as intermediary between giver and receiver. The Twelve intend to focus their attention on another type of διακονία, "the ministry of the word" (12:4). Since "the word" is the message from God, the Twelve portray themselves as administrators of this teaching, channels through which doctrine flows from God to the church. This parallels Paul's view that "ministry" or "service" occurs as individuals allow a talent or gift to come from God through themselves to the church, in the same way that benevolent funds would move from a donor through the Seven to those in need.

Within this broader framework of Paul's understanding of "service"/διακονία as a relationship between God, gift, and gifted person, it seems likely that the διάκονος of Philippians 1:1 and 1 Timothy 3 represents an institutionalization of giftedness. Persons exhibiting gifts which were particularly valuable to the life of the Pauline churches apparently received an official position of responsibility and authority after being

[3]This passage is included here under the assumption that the "we passages" of Acts suggest that the author/narrator of Acts desires to be associated with Pauline Christianity.

subjected to ethical scrutiny. The association of the deacon with the overseer in both contexts suggests a secondary, technical role, parallel to the relationship between the Twelve and the Seven in Acts 6. Like the apostles, Paul's overseers were responsible for the spiritual and pastoral care of the Christian community; Paul's deacons, like the Seven, presumably possessed the technical skills necessary to the accomplishment of the spiritual vision provided by the overseers. The specific functions and duties of each deacon would vary, depending on the particular service gifts which that individual possessed.

Within this framework, it may be said that every individual congregation within the modern church has "deacons," whether or not such a title is specifically used. Any person who has received any title based on the administration of a particular ability in the interests of the congregation would be, in Pauline terminology, a "deacon." Persons such as worship leaders, religious educators, choir directors, outreach directors, trustees, finance directors and treasurers, facilities maintenance directors, and youth leaders would all fall under the broad rubric of the Pauline "deacon." As recognized, titled servants of the congregation, such persons are called to exhibit not only "gifts" but also certain character traits. These traits are the subject of the next section.

2. *"Deacons Likewise Must Be. . ."*

While references to the function of deacons in the primitive church are rare, an extensive list of specific qualifications for the position appears at 1 Timothy 3:8–13. These qualifications are ethical, referring to both positive (attitudes and behaviors which must be present) and negative (attitudes and behaviors which must not be present) aspects of the candidate's lifestyle. Many modern churches interpret this passage as a specific moral absolute, using it literally as a "checklist" in the consideration of individuals nominated for the diaconate. The "checklist" approach often leads to frustration, as few candidates fulfill every specific qualification. For this reason, specific items from the list in 1 Timothy 3 are often canonized as essential, while others are overlooked. Churches might, for example, allow persons to be deacons who do not "hold the mystery of the faith with a clear conscience" (3:8) or do not exhibit strong family management (3:12), while forbidding any divorced person from holding this position. The latter strategy is common in American congregations, which often interpret "husband of one wife" (3:12; KJV, NASV, NIV) to mean that candidates cannot be divorced or in a second marriage, despite an ever-increasing percentage of divorced believers. "Husband of one wife" is also frequently applied to the gender question, leading to the stipulation that women cannot hold the title "deacon."

The subjection of candidates to investigations of ethical scrutiny was apparently a practice of the Pauline churches as well. 1 Timothy 3:10 indicates that candidates were to be "tested" (δοκιμάζω [*dokimazô*]) before installation and accepted only if found "irreproachable" (ἀνέγκλητος [*anengklêtos*]). It is doubtful, however, that Paul's churches understood 1 Timothy 3:8–12 as an absolute moral "checklist." Presumably, they would have recognized that this passage is organized by a common ancient rhetorical device, the "vice/virtue list."

The "vice/virtue list" is a form of synecdoche (part represents whole) typical of Greco-Roman moral rhetoric. This device is used when a speaker/author wishes to characterize a particular lifestyle as moral or immoral.[4] Here the moralist's vision of inner ethical perfection or depravity is expressed in a list of typical behaviors evident in the life of the perfect or depraved person. The Pauline letters are rife with vice/virtue lists, often combined to compare the Christian and non-Christian worlds. A familiar example appears at Galatians 3:19–22. Paul first describes the sensually-driven person by listing fifteen behaviors which typically proceed from this mindset (3:19–21). This is followed by a description of the person who "walks by the Spirit" (3:16), a list of nine virtues or "fruits of the Spirit" which the mature Christian should exhibit. Paul indicates that both lists are only general characterizations by concluding the vice list with the warning that "those who practice such things [= anything like the vices enumerated] will not inherit the kingdom," and by concluding the virtue list with the assurance that "against such things [as the fruits of the Spirit enumerated here] there is no law" (3:21, 23).

[4]See the convenient discussion and examples in Abraham J. Malherbe, *Moral Exhortation: A Greco-Roman Sourcebook* (Library of Early Christianity 4; Philadelphia: Westminster, 1986) 138–41. A striking example of a vice list from the Jewish world appears in Philo of Alexandria's *Sacrifices of Cain and Abel* 32, which delineates 147 qualities of the "lover of pleasure."

Surely the Galatians, and modern believers, could add more "deeds of the flesh" and more "fruits of the Spirit" to these lists, and Paul invites them to do so in their Christian lives. The same rhetorical pattern appears in Colossians 3. A number of sinful attitudes and behaviors which believers are to "put aside" are listed in 3:5–9, while 3:12–17 describes the life of the person "chosen by God" by listing a variety of the virtues which such persons typically possess. A somewhat different application of the vice list appears in 1 Timothy 1:6–10, where the person under Law is characterized by fourteen vices which conclude with the summary item, "anything else contrary to sound teaching" (1:10). The Ephesians (1 Timothy 1:3) are left to determine what this "anything else" might be, but, in any case, the point has been made.

The open-ended nature of Paul's vice/virtue lists is important to the application of 1 Timothy 3:8–12. Rather than a checklist, this passage presents a number of standard virtues which the deacon should exhibit and character flaws which the deacon should not exhibit. This list could be expanded or contracted in various scenarios, depending upon the individual candidate under consideration. The ad hoc nature of such lists in Pauline rhetoric explains the discrepancy between the lists of qualifications for the overseer/elder at 1 Timothy 3:1–7 and Titus 1:5–9. Both passages stipulate that the overseer/elder must be above reproach, "husband of one wife," prudent (σώφρων [*sôphrôn*]), hospitable (φιλόξενος [*philoxenos*]), and in control of family and household, and must not be addicted to wine (μὴ πάροινος [*mê paroinos*]) or pugnacious (μὴ πλήκτης [*mê plêktês*]). Titus alone, however, mentions that the overseer/elder must be a lover of good (φιλάγαθος [*philagathos*]), just (δίκιαος [*dikaios*]), pious (ὅσιος [*hosios*]), self-controlled (ἐγκρατής [*egkratês*]), not self-willed (μὴ αὐθάδης [*mê authadês*]), not short tempered (μὴ ὀργίλος [*mê orgilos*]), and not desirous of sordid gain (μὴ αἰσχροκερδής [*mê aischrokerdês*], applied to deacons at 1 Tim 3:8), while 1 Timothy alone insists such persons be temperate (νηφάλιος [*nêphalios*]), respectable (κόσμιος [*kosmios*]), uncontentious (ἄμαχος [*amachos*]), not lovers of money (ἀφιλάργυρος [*aphilarguros*]), and not new converts. Rather than an inconsistency, this discrepancy reflects the broad behavioral spectrum through which the underlying Pauline character profile for overseers/elders could be expressed. The same breadth of specific vices and virtues is evident in all Pauline usages of the vice/virtue list, including the list of qualifications for deacons at 1 Timothy 3:8–12. Theoretically, a character flaw in any one specific item in this list would only disqualify a candidate for deacon if such flaw indicated an inconsistency with the broader underlying profile.

But if 1 Timothy 3:8–12 does not represent a checklist of specific essential character traits, what underlying character profile does it represent? In other words, what kind of person should the deacon be? The answer may be found in the summary statement of 1 Timothy 3:10. Candidates whose character has been "tested" must be found "beyond reproach" (NASV), or, as the NIV translates, must have "nothing against them." The KJV refers to this person as "blameless." "Blamelessness," being possessed of a character which does not lend itself to criticism or accusation, is also the foremost characteristic of the Pauline elder. The lists of qualifications for the overseer/elder at 1 Timothy 3:2 and Titus 1:6 both begin by stressing that the elder/overseer's character is above accusation, particularly the sort of accusation which might discredit the position or, more significantly, the church. The Pastoral Epistles evidence throughout a particular concern that the church's reputation not be damaged by the behavior of its members. Titus 2:8, for example, urges "young men" to exhibit good deeds and sound speech so that enemies of the church will have no ammunition for slander, and 2:10 calls believing slaves to honesty so that masters will appreciate Christian teaching. Because immoral behavior among leaders is particularly damaging to the church's reputation, careful instructions are provided in 1 Timothy 5:17–25 for the impeachment of wayward elders. The deacon, as a titled servant of the church with recognized abilities and responsibilities, must possess a character which will not bring shame to the church or to the position itself. Obviously, each culture has different standards for judging which character traits make an individual "blameless," and these standards should be considered in applying the specific qualifications indicated at 1 Timothy 3:8–12.

Within the broader profile of "blamelessness," the specific qualifications at 1 Timothy 3:8–12 suggest two comprehensive character traits in the Pauline profile of the deacon. Tom Friskney describes these traits as "faithfulness" and "responsibility." The deacon's marital life (3:12) indicates one's level of faithfulness and commitment, as does integrity in speech (3:8). Qualities such as "dignity," control over alcohol consumption, and refusal to pursue dishonest financial advancement (3:8) indicate that the candidate is a responsible person. The major testing ground for personal responsibility is the household, under the Pauline dictum if one is not capable of managing one's own household, one is not capable of managing God's household (3:5). If the deacon has children, good parenting skills are an indication of responsible character; but even without children, the management of one's personal affairs and household are a good indicator of the inner person. Other criteria might be applied to the "test" which are judged to be signs of faithfulness and responsibility in a specific culture, such as business practices and involvement in various social organizations. Faithfulness and responsibility are logically necessary qualities in persons entrusted with specific service responsibilities in the congregation. As such, the church must be certain that deacons are capable of executing these responsibilities in a way which will not embarrass themselves or the church.

It would seem, then, that deacons in the Pauline church were persons whom the church recognized as possessed of service gifts. When gifted persons were placed in positions of responsibility, their personal lives were apparently scrutinized to determine if they possessed prerequisite character traits. Aside from basic moral qualities, these character traits were primarily faithfulness and responsibility, traits necessary to insure successful execution of duties while avoiding the reproach of others both within and without the Christian community.

3. Can Deacons Be Divorced?

The prominence of divorce in contemporary Western culture has forced denominations and individual congregations to seriously consider whether divorced persons can hold certain leadership positions in the church. Many congregations have concluded that persons holding the title "deacon" cannot be divorced, primarily on the basis of 1 Timothy 3:8, which suggests that the deacon must be "the husband of one wife." It is often assumed that this qualification indicates that deacons a) cannot be single; b) cannot be divorced; and c) cannot be in a second marriage. As noted earlier, many congregations apply this criterion rigorously, so that divorced persons who exhibit particular gifts and who are otherwise "blameless" are not permitted to hold the title "deacon."

It is important to note, however, that "husband of one wife" is not necessarily a reference to divorce. The Greek phrase, μιᾶς γυναικὸς ἀνήρ [*mias gunaikos anêr*], literally "a one-woman man," is subject to at least five different interpretations.[5] First, it could simply indicate that the deacon must be married rather than single. This interpretation, however, seems unlikely, as the emphasis of the phrase seems to rest on the first term, "one," rather than upon the fact of marriage. It may be that this test applies only to married persons: if a deacon is married, that person must be a "one-woman man." Second, the phrase could be a prohibition against polygamy, meaning that the deacon could have no more than one wife at a time. While this interpretation is faithful to the phrase's emphasis on "one woman," it is unlikely in light of the cultural milieu of 1 Timothy. Gordon Fee notes that "polygamy was such a rare feature of pagan society that such a prohibition would function as a near irrelevancy."[6] Third, "one-woman man" could refer to persons who have remarried after the death of a spouse. This interpretation, however, is inconsistent with the Pauline view that widows and widowers are free to marry, as long as the new partner is also a believer (1 Cor 7:39; 1 Tim 5:14). A fourth interpretation sees the phrase as a prohibition against divorce. While this interpretation is reasonable, Towner notes that "there is no first-century evidence of its [this phrase's] use in connection with divorce"; in other words, if "one-woman man" does refer to persons who are not divorced, the term is unique to the Pauline literature, appearing in no other ancient author.[7] Finally, "one-woman man" could refer to marital faithfulness. This interpretation emphasizes the need for church officers to remain monogamous and faithful to their spouses.

---

[5]See Gordon D. Fee, *1 and 2 Timothy, Titus* (New International Bible Commentary; Peabody, MA: Hendrickson, 1988) 80–81, and Philip H. Towner, *1–2 Timothy & Titus* (InterVarsity Press New Testament Commentary Series; Downers Grove, IL: InterVarsity Press, 1994) 84–85.

[6]Fee, NIBC, 80; see also Towner, IVPNT, 84.

[7]Towner, IVPNT, 85.

While "one-woman man" at 1 Timothy 3:12 might reasonably indicate that the deacon cannot be divorced, the last option above, that the phrase refers to marital faithfulness, seems more likely. Two considerations support this conclusion. First, as noted earlier, the overall context of 1 Timothy 3:8–12 seeks to portray the outward signs of a faithful and responsible person. The marriage relationship is an obvious arena in which faithfulness and commitment are revealed. Presumably, if a person has light regard for the vows and responsibilities of marriage, this person might not possess the commitment and loyalty necessary for successful leadership in the church.

The second consideration relates to the phrase itself, μιᾶς γυναικὸς ἀνήρ, "a one-woman man." The problem of widows is addressed at 1 Timothy 5:1–15, specifically the issue of whether or not the church should provide financial assistance to the bereaved. This discussion includes a virtue list which profiles the character of the kind of widow who may receive such assistance (5:9–10). Among these virtues, the candidate for aid must be ἑνὸς ἀνδρὸς γυνή (*henos andros gunê*), "a one man woman." This phrase is linguistically parallel to "one-woman man," reversing only the genders of the parties involved. Since a widow, by definition, is neither married nor divorced, the phrase "one-man woman" must refer to her faithfulness to her husband before his death. Since "one-woman man" at 1 Timothy 3:12 is parallel to this usage, and in light of the broader context of 1 Timothy 3, it seems doubtful that "husband of one wife" is a blanket prohibition against all divorced persons receiving the title "deacon."

While "husband of one wife" does not prohibit divorced persons from serving as deacons, it nevertheless advises caution in the examination of divorced candidates. In the case of a divorced candidate, the church must determine whether the candidate caused the divorce through unfaithfulness or was victimized by an unfaithful spouse. "Unfaithfulness" in this context is not limited to sexual impropriety. If the divorced candidate handled the marriage relationship irresponsibly, the congregation must consider carefully that person's ability to handle positions of leadership and responsibility in any voluntary body such as a church. If, however, the candidate was faithful to the former spouse and hence not responsible for the divorce, the Pauline dictum that the wronged partner "is not bound" (1 Cor 7:15) would seem to apply. In every case, the church should judge each candidate as an individual, not as a member of a stereotypical category.

4. "The Women Also…"

The changing roles of women in Western society have forced every denomination and congregation to reevaluate the roles of women in the church. While a full treatment of the nuances of this issue is beyond the scope of the present study, it is necessary to consider whether women did or did not serve as "deacons" in the Pauline church. Two verses will be particularly relevant to this investigation, Romans 16:1 and 1 Timothy 3:11.

The book of Romans closes with a long series of greetings to members of the church at Rome. This greeting section begins with a recommendation that the Romans receive and assist Phoebe, a Christian woman from Cenchrea (Corinth) who has assisted Paul and a number of believers (16:2). In his recommendation, Paul refers to Phoebe as "our sister" and as διάκονον τῆς ἐκκλησίας (*diakonon tês ekklesias*) in Cenchrea. The KJV, NASV, and NIV all translate the latter phrase, "a servant of the church which is at Cenchrea." "Servant" here is διάκονος, the same term used of deacons at Philippians 1:1 and 1 Timothy 3:8–13. Does Paul's use of διάκονος at Romans 16:1 imply that Phoebe held the title "deacon," or, as the KJV, NASV, and NIV suggest, does it mean that Phoebe was simply a gifted person who exercised her gifts in service to believers?

The Greek text provides clues for resolving this problem. Unlike English, the Greek language, like French or German, differentiates words on the basis of gender: words which apply to males take one form, while words which apply to females take a different form. The word διάκονος is masculine, suggesting that it should normally be applied only to males. At Romans 16:1, however, Paul applies this term to Phoebe, a woman. Such usage is grammatically inaccurate, similar to the modern English usage, "Joan is chairman of the Building Committee." The phrase, "Joan is chairman," does not suggest that Joan is a "man," but rather indicates that "chairman" is a technical title for the position Joan holds. The same would seem to be the case with Phoebe. Although Phoebe is obviously a woman, Paul uses the masculine term διάκονος, "deacon," to describe her because she holds this official title in the church at Cenchrea. The NASV recognizes this with the somewhat clumsy marginal reading "deaconess," an English-language feminine form of "deacon" which has no corresponding Greek term. Had Paul wished to refer to Phoebe simply as a person who used her gifts for service, an attributive participle of the verb διακονέω would have been more appropriate, producing the English reading, "Phoebe, one who serves the church at Cenchrea." As the text of Romans 16:1 stands, Paul's reference to Phoebe as "sister" and "deacon" indicates both her membership and position in the Cenchrean church.

This reference to Phoebe sheds light on the problematic 1 Timothy 3:11, which interrupts the list of qualifications for deacons to discuss "women likewise" (γυναῖκας ὡσαύτως [*gunaikas hôsautôs*]). While the NASV retains the literal translation, the KJV and NIV translate this phrase, "their wives also," implying that the church should also scrutinize the character of the spouse of the male candidate for deacon. The difficulty in this case arises from the fact that the Greek word γυνή can mean "wife" specifically or "woman" generically. Both the KJV and NIV translate this term as "woman" rather than "wife" five times in 1 Timothy 2:9–15, the passage immediately preceding discussion of overseers and deacons. The shift to "wives" at 3:11 apparently reflects the translators' view that women did not serve as deacons in the Pauline church. It seems more likely, however, that the "women" referred to at 3:11 are females who, like Phoebe, hold the title "deacon." This explains both the sudden intrusion of 3:11 into the overall discussion of 3:8–13, and the fact that 1 Timothy 3:1–7 and Titus 1:5–9 do not call the church to scrutinize the wife of the overseer/elder. Obviously, a supportive spouse is critical to success in any service position, whether the servant is male or female. 1 Timothy 3:11, however, more likely refers to qualities which a female deacon should particularly possess, primarily again "faithfulness in all things."[8]

---

[8]The few qualities mentioned, "dignity," "not a gossip," "temperate," are consistent with 1 Tim 2:9–15 and reflect generic Greco-Roman images of the virtuous woman; see examples in Malherbe, *Moral Exhortation* 82–85, 97–102, 132–34. For detailed discussion of 1 Tim 3:11, see Jennifer H. Stiefel, "Woman Deacons in 1 Timothy: A Linguistic

5. Why Be a Deacon?

Confusion over duties and hesitance to submit to ethical scrutiny lead many to decline nominations for the diaconate. In many congregations, untitled individuals can serve just as effectively, perhaps even more effectively, than "deacons," while avoiding the congregational politics in which deacons are often embroiled. Appropriately, 1 Timothy 3:8–13 closes with a word of assurance to those who accept the title "deacon." Deacons who serve well receive recognition from both the church and God, a "high standing" among God's people and "great confidence in faith" that God will recognize and reward their efforts. While one should not accept the position only for prestige or in hopes of receiving divine blessing, the "fringe benefits" of the work make it well worth the effort.

Any person who is offered a titled position of responsibility, whether that title includes the word "deacon" or not, should reflect carefully on two factors in his or her personal life. First, one must consider the position offered and honestly evaluate whether one has the "gifts" necessary to fulfill the responsibility. While this rule normally applies to persons who lack ability but desire prestige, it is also calls gifted persons who "don't want the hassle" to reflect on the abilities God has graciously given. Second, one must consider one's own character, reflecting honestly on the questions, "Am I a faithful person? Am I responsible and reliable? Do my attitudes and behavior reveal the kind of character which will not bring shame to myself or the church?" While this reflection need not involve a "checklist" of virtues, it demands that candidates neither overestimate nor underestimate their inner life. While many people hold the title "deacon" who are certainly not qualified for that position, the greater tragedy lies in those capable persons who refuse to do what they should.

---

and Literary Look at 'Women Likewise…' (1 Tim 3.11)," *New Testament Studies* 41 (1995) 442–457.

CHAPTER 6

Symbolic Numbers in Scripture

LARRY PECHAWER

Much of the confusion in various attempts to interpret Bible prophecy stems from the failure to handle figurative language correctly. My "basic training" in the study of figurative language in the Bible came primarily through courses taught by Professor Thomas Friskney. I learned to distinguish between the "thing" and the "kind of thing." I gained the insight that "non-literal" does not equal "non-existent." That is to say, realities, albeit not always physical ones, exist behind the symbolic language of Scripture. To "spiritualize" something is not to deny its reality. The handling of figurative language is aided by a sharp linguistic eye, a feel for literary styles, and a keen imagination. Professor Friskney proved in class that he had "the right stuff," including an added measure of patience and grace.

Figurative language is both natural and necessary. Milton Terry has suggested:

> Were we to suppose a language sufficiently copious in words to express all possible conceptions, the human mind would still require us to compare and contrast our concepts, and such a procedure would soon necessitate a variety of figures of speech. So much of our knowledge is acquired through the senses, that all our abstract ideas and our spiritual language have a material basis.[1]

There are numerous instances in which the ideas and concepts dealt with can only be conveyed by the use of figurative language. God has revealed spiritual truths clothed in language borrowed from material

---

[1] Milton Terry, *Biblical Hermeneutics: A Treatise on the Interpretation of the Old and New Testaments* (New York: Eaton & Mains, 1911) 244.

things. He has expressed the unknown in terms of the known. The Old Testament prophets could only speak of future glories of spiritual blessings in terms of their own times. And so one finds prophecies clothed in language utilizing past historical events known to the prophet and embracing the cultural and religious conditions and institutions of his day. The claim is made by premillennial dispensationalists that there are no direct prophecies of the church in the Old Testament (but there are!). It only needs to be said at this point that if there were indeed such prophecies, one would expect them to incorporate the outer trappings of the dispensation in which they were written (land, Levites, sacrifices, military conquest, covenant, monarchy, etc.). Had the Old Testament prophets been granted the words to convey the richness and fullness of the New Testament language and concepts, it would have been meaningless, and indeed confusing, to the Old Testament saints. As W. J. Grier explains, "They could not have borne such excess of light."[2]

A topic scantily covered in most hermeneutics texts is that of the symbolism behind various numbers in Scripture. Premillennial writers are especially terse in their treatments, owing in great part to their insistence on literal fulfillment to many prophecies, particularly those involving Israel. Numbers like "7," "12," and "40" are regularly noted, and of course there is "666." But for the most part, the significance for interpretation of the wide range of special numbers utilized in Scripture is left unaddressed. In this overview, we want to identify the basic symbolic numbers employed in the Bible and the rationale for declaring them symbolic. We want to differentiate between different kinds of symbolic numbers and the range of symbolism that a given number might convey. We would like to establish some guidelines for determining whether or not a number is symbolic in a given context. At the end of the presentation, we shall pay special attention to symbolic numbers found in the Book of Revelation as a case study for some of the methodology to be suggested below.

---

[2] W. J. Grier, *The Momentous Event: A Discussion of Scripture Teaching on the Second Advent* (London: Banner of Truth Trust, 1970) 39.

1. Mystical or "Encoded" Numbers

We need to distinguish from the outset between divinely-intentioned symbolism found in many numbers in Scripture, and the supposed mathematical properties found in the Bible by imaginative human interpreters. Both the Hebrew and Greek alphabets possess numerical equivalents for the various letters. In Hebrew, *aleph* = 1, *beth* = 2, ... *yod* = 10, ... *mem* = 40, etc. In medieval Judaism, a system knows as Gematria developed in which numerical values of words or phrases were used as aids to exegesis (in fact, eisegesis—reading *into* the text). "Shiloh comes" (Gen 49:10) was argued to be a Messianic prophecy (it is one, for other reasons!) because the numerical value of both "Shiloh comes" and the word "Messiah" is 358. The three messengers who visited Abraham (Gen 18:2) were identified by Jewish numericists as being Michael, Gabriel and Raphael (the last one being found in Jewish apocryphal writings). The interpretive key? The phrases "three men who stood by him" and "these are Michael, Gabriel, and Raphael" both have a numerical value of 701. And so it went in the practice of Gematria.

A modern version of such interpretive shenanigans can be found plastered over the internet, aided now by modern computer search programs. A book co-authored by the famous basketball star, Jerry Lucas, appeared in 1977.[3] *Theomatics* claimed that identical letter-number equivalencies demonstrate amazing divinely-encoded patterns in Scripture, especially in the New Testament. The other co-author, Del Washburn, was the real author of the book, with Jerry Lucas being the author of a brief "Foreword," and serving as Washburn's "spiritual supporter and advisor." Space does not permit a full critique, but much of the "remarkable" result of the painstaking research is clearly derived from an arbitrary selection of word combinations.

Here are a few examples of the kinds of results found in *Theomatics* (and Washburn's expanded version, *Theomatics II*).[4] Since 666, e.g., represents the number of the "Beast" in Revelation 13:10, Washburn looks

---

[3] Jerry Lucas and Del Washburn, *Theomatics: God's Best Kept Secret Revealed* (Briarcliff Manor, NY: Stein and Day, 1977).

[4] Del Washburn, *Theomatics II: God's Best Kept Secret Revealed* (Lanham, MD: Scarborough House, 1994).

for "666" multiples in passages relating to the "antichrist," Satan, etc. What results is a hodgepodge of equivalencies: "the man who bore the mark" (Rev 16:2) = 666 × 9; "Those who worship the beast and its image" (Rev 14:11) = 666 × 6; "The one who has the mark, or the name of the beast, or the number of its name" (Rev 13:17) = 666 × 11, etc. Since "Jesus" = 888, Washburn looks for the patterns involving 888 ("her begotten" [Matt 1:20]) and also 111 (111 × 8 = 888) and 37 (37 × 3 = 111)! We "find" such phenomena as: "And she will bear a son" (Matt 1:21) = 111 × 11; "She bore a son and called the name of Him Jesus" (Matt 1:25) = 111 × 34; "This child" (Luke 2:17) = 111 × 26; "We have found the Messiah" (John 1:41) = 37 × 42; "The Messiah" (John 1:41) = 37 × 25; "Christ" (in the Greek accusative case) = 111 × 12; "Lord" (in the genitive case) = 111 × 9; "Lord God" (nominative case) = 888. In fairness to Washburn, these are just a handful of many examples he offers. On the other hand, it is fairly obvious that many of the "matches" are due to arbitrary selections of words and phrases. Three, four, five, ten words can be strung together to make it work. And of course the inflected nature of the Greek language enables a given word to have dozens of different forms, each with its own numerical value. The possibilities are endless!

In my view, these approaches are dead ends, the alleged "divine pattern" being rather a human imposition. Unfortunately, this approach continues to be taught as an apologetic tool that bears witness to the divine origin of Scripture.

The same is true of the misguided Bible Code efforts that claim to find divinely-encoded messages in the Bible by doing computer-aided searches of words or phrases by skipping a set number of letters (called equidistant letter searches [ELS]). This approach has hit mainstream attention with the publication of Michael Drosnin's best-selling book, *The Bible Code.*[5] This approach to finding "hidden messages" in the Bible is invalid for a number of reasons. It is also dangerous, as it borders on divination and magic. It makes a claim for the Bible that is erroneous and misleading, and sends enticed Christians down a path that leads to confusion and disappointment. Even many unbelievers are caught up in it (including Drosnin), people who care nothing for what the Bible teaches

[5] Michael Drosnin, *The Bible Code* (New York: Simon & Schuster, 1997).

"on the surface," but are fascinated by the submerged, "encoded" message brought to light by ELS. One point of refutation involves the spelling practices of ancient Hebrew and Aramaic, the languages of the Old Testament. The use of certain consonants to represent vowel signs was a frequent, but inconsistent, practice in Biblical Hebrew. The word "generations" (*toledoth*) is spelled four different ways in Genesis! These spelling variations do not affect the meaning of the words in any way, but they wreak havoc on equidistant letter searches, since the exact sequence of letters is critical to the search results. The spelling of the medieval Rabbinic Bible used for "Bible Code" searches simply does not represent the original spelling of the Biblical text, as all Old Testament scholars agree. This invalidates the entire approach, irrespective of other arguments against it.

2. Kinds of Symbolic Numbers

Another expression for "symbolic" number could be the term *qualitative* number. Qualitative numbers signify the *quality* and not the precise *quantity* of a thing. Numbers that denote perfection or completeness—like the numbers 7, 10, 12, 40, or 1,000—are used with great frequency in Scripture. They should be studied from the broader perspective of how such numbers function in Biblical literature as a whole, before they are plugged into various prophetic schemes and dreams. As a prominent example, the number "1,000" often serves as a large, qualitative number in Scripture. It may speak to a large, limited amount in some contexts, or it can convey a limitless, unending quality.

2.1. Stylistic or Rhetorical Numbers

A numerical literary formula frequently found in the Old Testament (and in other ancient Semitic texts) is the x…x + 1 device in which a sequence of numbers is utilized to produce the stylistic effect of intensification or climactic progression. Amos' famous "for three transgressions, yea for four" thunders throughout the first two chapters of his book. Yet we find that many different combinations exist, among them: 2…3 (Isa 17:6); 3…4 (Deut 5:9; Amos 1:3–2:6; Prov 30:15, 18, etc.); 4…5 (Isa 17:6); 5…6 (2 Kgs 13:19); 6…7 (Prov 6:16; Job 5:19); 7…8 (Mic 5:4).

In many of the above and similar cases, the precise numbers chosen do not seem to be critical to the point, rather it is the formulation x...x + 1 that primarily serves to produce the desired effect.

We also note the sequence x...10x in "Saul has slain his thousands, but David his ten thousands" (1 Sam 18:7, etc.). Psalm 91:7 reads, "A thousand may fall at your side, and ten thousand at your right hand" (cf. Deut 32:30; Mic 6:7). Many similar examples of x...x + 1 and x...10x can be found in the Canaanite inscriptions from the ancient coastal city of Ugarit (c. 1300 B.C.). Additional combinations exist such as 66...77 (11x...11[x + 1]) or 80...90 (10x...10[x + 1]), among others.[6] Also, several times in both the Old and New Testaments we find combinations of "one or two" or "two or three" that seem to designate the basic notion of "a few" or "small in number" (Judg 5:30; 2 Kgs 9:32; Deut 17:6; Amos 4:8; Matt 18:20; John 2:6).

2.2. Perfect/Complete Numbers

The so-called "divine number," the number "7" is best viewed as a number denoting perfection or completeness. Used extensively to describe things pertaining to God and worship, "7" is also used in a broad range of contexts. It is found in frequent references outside the Bible, e.g., in Canaanite, Babylonian, and Sumerian literature, often in the sense of "all," or "complete."

Within the parameters of the Mosaic system, we find "7" in reference to sacrificial regulations, lengths of feasts, the sabbath day, sabbath year, and Year of Jubilee (following a 7 × 7 cycle). Among historical narratives, we find Jacob serving 7 years for Rachel (Gen 29:20–28); 7 years of plenty and 7 years of famine (Gen 41:53, 54); 7 sons of Jesse (1 Sam 16:10); 7 sons of Saul (2 Sam 21:6); Naaman dipped 7 times in the Jordan (2 Kgs 5:10); Jericho encircled 7 days, 7 times on the 7th day, with 7 priests carrying 7 trumpets before the ark (Josh 6:4). Cain's murder would be avenged 7-fold (Gen 4:24); silver refined 7 times in the furnace is pure (Ps 12:6); God is praised by the psalmist 7 times a day

[6] See H. L. Ginsberg in J. B. Pritchard, *Ancient Near Eastern Texts Relating to the Old Testament* (Princeton, NJ: Princeton University Press, 1969) 129–155.

(Ps 119:164). Many other examples could of course be cited, and some will be examined in our discussion of the book of Revelation.

But what makes the number “7” itself symbolic, representing the idea of being full or complete? The simplest answer is that it points to the 7-day cycle of a week. This week is grounded in the order of creation revealed in the first chapters of Genesis. The 7-day week represents God’s completed work of creation, and serves to mark a recurring cycle.

The cyclical nature of “7” would also seem to be a key in understanding the “completion / perfection” imagery found in other numbers, such as “12,” “30,” or “40.” In the case of “12,” the obvious foundational basis for the symbolic imagery would be the 12 sons of Jacob/12 tribes of Israel (noting that they *are* different!) Numerous items are in groups of 12 because of this connection: pillars (Exod 24:4); stones (Exod 28:21); yoke of oxen (1 Kgs 19:19); pieces of garment (1 Kgs 11:40); body parts (Judg 19:29); thrones (Matt 19:28); various sacrifices, altars, etc., to which are added the frequent images in the book of Revelation.

But then the question becomes, why *12* sons/tribes? While recognizing that there needs to be no definitive answer, I understand the 12 months of the calendar year as being foundational here, 12 months comprising a complete cycle. Among some of the other references to “12” in Scripture we find several pointing to a chronological completeness. Nebuchadnezzar’s malady occurred 12 months after the ominous dream (Dan 4:29); Jesus speaks of the 12 hours in a day (John 11:9); Revelation 22:2 describes the tree of life bearing 12 kinds of fruit, each in its mouth. Other references seem to be in connection with the idea of the “people of God,” but not always in a strict sense. There were 12 baskets full after 5,000 were fed (Matt 14:20); Jesus could have called 12 legions of angels to his aid (Matt 26:53). Of course the 12 apostles serve as the New Testament correspondence to the “12” imagery for Israel.

The nature of “12” as a complete number is also seen in the Jewish custom that declared a male child a man (a “son of the covenant”) upon reaching age 13. The span of 12 years was thus completed, and a new phase began (*Mishnah*, tractate *Aboth* (“Fathers”), 5.21). We find Jesus at age 12 on a pilgrimage to observe the festive rites just prior to this milestone in his life, as rabbinic law enjoined (Luke 2:42).

Numbers like "30" and "40" might be viewed as having their symbolic significance based on a cyclical model as well. A month of 30 days provides another cyclical pattern of completion. Age 30 was significant for manhood, priestly ministry, etc. Joseph was 30 when he stood before Pharaoh (Gen 41:46); David became king at age 30 (as did possibly Saul); 30 shekels was the price of a slave (Exod 21:32); Israel wept 30 days for Aaron (Num 20:29) and Moses (Deut 34:8); prayer in Babylon was prohibited for 30 days (Dan 6:7, 12); Esther had not been summoned for 30 days (Esth 4:11); Samson had 30 companions at his feast (Judg 14:11); David had his select group of 30 chieftains (2 Sam 23:13), etc. Interestingly, the listing of David's "30" ends with the summation, "thirty-seven in all" (2 Sam 23:39). The "30" designation may have become a rubric, not a literal grouping. On the other hand, the "thirty-seven in all" may represent some who died in their service with the "30" and were replaced by others.

The number "40" functions as a complete period, stemming from its connection to the concept of a "generation," although that specific connection in Scripture is pretty much limited to the Wilderness Wandering period. In many passages with the number "40," a time of testing or endurance seems to be involved. During the Noahic flood it rained 40 days and nights (Gen 7:4, 12, 17); both Isaac and his son Esau were 40 when they married (Gen 25:20; 26:34); 40 days were required for the embalming of Jacob (Gen 50:3); 40 stripes was the limit to the beating that could be inflicted from a judicial ruling (Deut 25:3); Goliath presented himself before Israel for 40 days (1 Sam 17:16); the "iniquity of Judah" was assigned to be 40 days/years (Ezek 4:6); the period of probation announced by Jonah for Nineveh was 40 days (Jonah 3:4); periods of fasting lasted 40 days for Moses, Elijah, and Jesus (Exod 24:18; 1 Kgs 19:8; Matt 4:2); Jesus was tempted of the devil 40 days (Luke 4:2); Jesus presented himself alive after his resurrection over a period of 40 days (Acts 1:3). In many of the examples cited, chronological spans are involved, and they should be taken literally, with a reasonable degree of rounding off, unless there is strong evidence to the contrary.

Mention must be made of the various extensions of such "perfect" numbers. From the numbers 7, 12, 30, 40, we find multiples and extensions such as 70, 7,000, 120, 12,000, 48, 72, 96, 300, 3,000, 400, 4,000, etc. In a notable example God reminded Elijah that there were left in Israel yet 7,000 who had not bowed the knee to Baal (1 Kgs 19:18; Rom 11:4). At Ezra 8:35 we find "12" imagery in the sacrifices being offered: 12 bulls, 96 rams, 77 lambs, and 12 male goats. The number 77 is somewhat curious. Although itself a type of "perfect" number, we would expect from the context the multiple of 12, "72," just as we have the multiple "96." Evidence for the number "72" here, however, exists in the apocryphal 1 Esdras, an embellished recounting of Ezra and Nehemiah. The Jewish historian Josephus follows 1 Esdras in his account here in his *Antiquities of the Jews,* and thus also has 72 lambs being offered (11.5.2). Further support for this textual variant is found in the paleography (shapes of letters) of fifth-century Hebrew and Aramaic inscriptions. In Jewish papyri found from the time of Ezra and Nehemiah the words "seven" and "two" are extremely similar in appearance. In my view the original reading of the Hebrew text was likely "72." Thus we find the phenomenon of number symbolism serving as a clue in text-critical issues.

Another issue to consider is the status of other numbers such as "3," "4," "5," "6," etc. Caution here should be exercised. A classic approach to avoid is that of E. W. Bullinger.[7] Bullinger (1837–1913) noted that with "3" we come to the first geometrical figure. "3" conveys solid objects; therefore, it stands for what is solid, real, complete, entire. It also seems to mark deity. "4" is 3 + 1 and thus points to creation coming from God. "4" has reference to all that is created. "5" is 4 + 1 and is the number of "grace" since it involves adding divine strength to man's weakness. "6" is the number of "man," and represents either 4 + 2 (man's world + man's enmity to God) *or* 5 + 1 (God's grace made of none effect by man's addition to it, or corruption of it). Bullinger's list goes on and on, and serves as an unfortunate prelude to some of the more recent *Gematria/Theomatics* approaches.

In the case of the numbers "3" and "4," some exploration is warranted. The "Trinity" evokes much 3-fold imagery in Scripture, including the "Holy, holy, holy" of Isa 6:3. We also should at least concede that

---

[7] E. W. Bullinger, *Number in Scripture: Its Supernatural Design and Spiritual Significance* (reprint; Grand Rapids: Kregel, 1971 [= 1894]).

both time and space are 3-fold. As well, the material universe is generally delineated in Scripture as comprised of the heavens, earth, and sea. In my estimation, however, "30" as a qualitative symbol should not be viewed as an extension of "3," since it has a clear cyclical pattern of its own.

The number "4" does seem to convey the idea of the created earth, primarily from the aspect of direction. We read of the 4 corners of the earth (Isa 11:12; Ezra 7:2); the 4 winds of heaven (Dan 7:2; Zech 2:6; Matt 24:31); the 4 living creatures before the throne, facing all sides (Rev 4:6 ff.; Ezra 1:5–21). We should add to this the fact that the New Jerusalem is described as being "foursquare" (Rev 21:16). Again, however, we should resist the supposition that "40," itself a symbol for a generation-period, is somehow an extension of "4."

2.3. Rounded/Complete Numbers

The utilization of a decimal system in the Hebrew and Greek cultures serves as the basic explanation why numbers like "10," "100," "1,000" and "10,000" and various multiples of each take on a qualitative status in Scripture, just as they do in modern English and other languages. How many times have *you* been "told a 1,000 times" about something? We talk about an item costing $40–50, not $42–52. Boxers need to be up by the count of 10. The word "decimate" originally meant to exact or destroy a tenth, but it now refers to widespread destruction.

The number "10" in Scripture is a two-edged sword. It generally denotes a small rounded number, yet in contexts where "few" is the norm, it can represent a large qualitative amount (10 hours in the dentist's chair is *huge*; 10 days' vacation, not so huge). Rebekah's brother and mother urged Abraham's servant to allow her to stay with family a little longer: "a few days, say ten" (Gen 24:55). Boaz took 10 men from the elders of the city (Ruth 4:2). We read of 10-stringed instruments (Ps 33:2; 92:3; 144:9), and 10 loaves and 10 cheeses being delivered by young David to the troops (1 Sam 17:17). King David left behind 10 concubines to keep his house when he fled from Absalom.

The number "10" can be viewed as a substantial quantity in certain contexts. "Am I not better to you than ten sons?" Elkanah asked in his efforts (unsuccessful!) to console Hannah (1 Sam 1:8). In a similar fashion, the number "7" is used when Naomi is told that Ruth was better to her "than seven sons" (Ruth 4:15). Daniel asked for his friends and himself to be proved 10 days regarding dietary practices (Dan 1:12–15), and eventually Nebuchadnezzar came to regard them as 10 times better than all the magicians and conjurers in his realm (Dan 1:20). Joab would have given 10 pieces of silver to the one who slew Absalom (2 Sam 18:11). Eccl 7:19 states, "Wisdom strengthens wise men more than ten rulers who are in a city." Job's friends at one point had insulted him "10 times" (Job 19:3). The Israelites who came out of Egypt had just put God to the test "10 times" (Num 14:22—the NASB editors here amassed marginal references in an apparent attempt to document "all 10"!). The Jews rebuilding Jerusalem's walls were told of the enemy threats "10 times" (Neh 4:12). The saints in Smyrna were to suffer tribulations "10 days" (Rev 2:10).

The proportion 10:1 indicates a substantial increase/decrease. Saul's "thousands" were overshadowed by David's "ten thousands." In Nehemiah's day, 1 in 10 were chosen by lot to dwell within the city limits of Jerusalem (Neh 11:1). Soldiers leaving Israel's cities 1,000 strong would return with only 100. Those leaving 100 strong would have remaining only 10 (Amos 5:3). In the captivities threatened Israel in case of future disobedience, 10 women would have to bake bread in one oven (Lev 26:26), while Israel was being punished "7 times for their sins" (Lev 26:24; cf. Isa 14:1, where "7 women" would be forced to beg for a husband following God's judgment on the nation). God tells Isaiah that a "tenth portion" would be left to God's people in connection with future captivity (Isa 6:13).

To conclude our discussion of the number "10," we must note in passing such obvious items as the 10 plagues on Egypt, the 10 Commandments, and the tithe or tenth portion. In such examples, a qualitative sense is clearly implied, even though 10 specific things are enumerated.

The number "1,000" provides controversy in at least two respects. First, some scholars have attempted to explain away some of the large numbers in the Old Testament (armies of 300,000, 700,000 or more, etc.) by suggesting that the Hebrew word *eleph*, "1,000," should really be understood as *alluph*, "tribal chief." Thus we find not 300,000 soldiers, but rather 300 chiefs (with their clans, tribes). This approach simply does not make sense or fit Scriptural claims in the vast majority of cases. In addition, we find rather significant numbers from other ancient sources regarding armies, captives taken, sacrificial offerings, royal banquets and entourages, etc.

The single passage that provides the most controversy regarding the number "1,000" is Revelation 20:1–6, where Satan is bound and Christ reigns for 1,000 years. We shall revisit that text, but for now we need to examine the numerous qualitative uses for the number "1,000" throughout Scripture.

Moses asked that God increase Israel a "thousand-fold" (Deut 1:11), the God who keeps His covenant and loving kindness to a "thousandth generation" (Deut 7:9; cf. 1 Chron 16:15; Ps 105:8). With God's help, one Israelite could put 1,000 enemies to flight (Deut 32:30; Josh 23:10; cf. Isa 30:17). God owns the cattle on 1,000 hills (Ps 50:10), and a day in His courts is better than 1,000 outside (Ps 84:10). 1,000 years in His sight are like yesterday when it passes by, for a day with the Lord is like 1,000 years (Ps 90:4; 2 Pet 3:8). What does it matter if a man lives 1,000 years twice (Eccl 6:6)? A wise man among 1,000 is hard to find (Eccl 7:28). In view of these references, it is quite natural to understand the "1,000 years" (Latin *millennium*) in Revelation 20 as a large qualitative number, especially since to take it literally is to create a 1,000-year period nowhere else specifically delineated in Scripture.

The number "10,000" is also noteworthy. The Hebrew/Aramaic *rebabah/ribbo* and Greek *myriades/myrioi*, all indicating "10,000," represent the largest simple numbers found in these languages. Larger amounts must be indicated by multiples of thousands and/or "myriads"/10,000's. "10,000" can be represented as a number itself or as a multiple of "1,000." The latter is the case when Joab asks David, "Are you not worth 10,000 of us?" (using "ten" plus "thousand"; 2 Sam 18:3). Both "1,000" and "10,000" can function as symbolic numbers, with "1,000" being much more common.

It might be helpful to note that the writing of numbers in the Hebrew and Greek Scriptures always utilized the spelling of words, and not numerical notations, e.g., "forty-six," not "46." It is true, however, that certain of the early Greek New Testament papyri (e.g., Chester Beatty Papyri) use the letter-number equivalencies in a few passages (they abbreviate certain common words like "Jesus" and "God" as well). From the fifth-century Aramaic papyri found in Egypt, we know that the Jews used a notation system to write numbers, but there is no proof that the Old Testament text ever used such a system. Some of the problems in the transmission of numbers in the Old Testament manuscripts are probably best explained, however, by the speculation that such a notation system was utilized at some phase.

2.4. "Signifying" Numbers

Beyond the category of "complete" numbers, there are numbers that are symbolic or significant because of an earlier reality attached to the number. This area of investigation can lead us into the realm of typology in which an Old Testament reality (*type*) points to a corresponding New Testament reality or "fulfillment" (*antitype*). A classic example of such a typical relationship would be Elijah and John the Baptist (Luke 1:17; Matt 11:9–15; 17:9–13).

2.4.1. The Number "3,000." There are certain numbers in the Bible that can take on a special significance, but not always typologically so, because of a specific historical circumstance or antecedent event. The fact that about 3,000 were baptized on the Day of Pentecost (Acts 2:41) takes on a new meaning when we remember that this event marks the beginning of "New Covenant Israel," and that on the day the Old Covenant was earlier offered to Israel, about 3,000 *died* as a result of disobedience (Exod 32:28). In a different context, Paul described the Old and New Covenants respectively as the "ministry of death" and the "ministry of the Spirit/life" (2 Cor 3:6–8).

Is this "3,000" correspondence an example of typology? What makes a typological relationship? The safest approach in my view is to limit our understanding of *types* and *antitypes* to those entities that are clearly connected by Scriptural statements. There is no clear connection indicated regarding the 3,000 at Sinai and the 3,000 later at Pentecost. Caution is therefore warranted. However, the notion that the 3,000 in Acts is a "signifying" number would drag it into the typology realm, since it would not have a "signifying" function were there not an earlier event to which it pointed. In other words, if the number *is* intended to point back to the corresponding Old Testament incident, then typology *does* exist. The numerical similarity, along with the similarity of the nature of the events involved, is at least suggestive of a designed similarity. In typology we are always dealing with *divine* design and intention, however, and without a specific statement in Scripture tying the two numbers together, we are left in the realm of opinion.

2.4.2. The Number "5." A clear example of a "signifying" and therefore symbolic number is the number "5." We do not think of "5" as normally being symbolic, but in one specific Biblical context it is. We read in 1 Samuel 6:4 that when the Philistines returned to the Israelites the ark of the covenant which they had earlier captured (1 Sam 4:11), they sent along a guilt offering of 5 golden "hemorrhoids"/lumps and 5 golden mice, "according to the number of the lords of the Philistines." Philistia was a confederation of 5 city-states: Ashdod, Ashkelon, Ekron, Gaza and Gath (1 Sam 6:17, 18). The power and extent of Philistia, then, was represented by the number "5." This gives new meaning to what we learn in 1 Samuel 17:40, where David chose for himself 5 smooth stones from the brook in preparation for his confrontation with Goliath. Why 5 stones? Perhaps it just happened to be the number of stones that looked particularly useful to David. Also possible, however, is that they represent the defeat of Philistia, the 5-fold confederacy threatening Israel's very existence (whether or not David so reasoned in his selection process).

Grant Jeffrey has another, less likely, explanation.[8] He argues that the 5 stones were selected by David in case 5 giants appeared, Goliath along with his four brothers! 2 Samuel 21:22 (note vv. 16–22) states that there were four giants born to "the giant" (Hebrew *rapha*) in Gath: Ishbi-benob (v. 16), Saph (v. 18; "Sippai" at 1 Chron 20:4), Lahmi (found in 1 Chron 20:5, but "lost" in 2 Sam 21:19 because of a later copyist error), and a fourth giant described as having six fingers on each hand and six toes on each foot (v. 20). The fact that Lahmi is described as the brother of Goliath (1 Chron 20:5) seems to indicate that these four giants were indeed brothers of Goliath. All 5 had in common that they were slain by David and his servants (v. 22).

---

[8] Grant Jeffrey, *The Signature of God: Astonishing Bible Discoveries* (Nashville: Word, 1996) 249–250.

Having said all this, it still seems unlikely that David grabbed 5 stones because "He might have needed the additional four stones to defeat the four other giants." However, here again the number 5 reasserts itself regarding Philistia. The vanquished hero giants of Philistia, Goliath and his brothers, were 5 in number. Coincidence?

2.4.3. The Number "430." The prophet Ezekiel performed a symbolic action in lying down on both his left and right sides for a prescribed period of days, days that represented the iniquity of the houses of Israel and Judah (Ezek 4:1–17). The prophet probably lay down for a portion of each day, perhaps the same general time period each day. He was to lie down 390 days on his left side for the iniquity of Israel, and 40 days on his right side for the iniquity of Judah. What was the symbolic value of these numbers?

We would note that the "iniquity period" likely concludes with the fall of Babylon in 539 B.C. Some 50,000 Jews returned home within a few years (538–536 B.C.). Jeremiah's 70 years of captivity arguably spans the years 605–536 B.C. (605 B.C. being the time of the first Babylonian deportation; Jer 25:11, 12; 29:10).

For Judah, we see a period of "iniquity" roughly equivalent to the 40+ years of captivity involving the time between the fall of Jerusalem (586 B.C.) and the fall of Babylon (539 B.C.). For Israel, the iniquity/captivity began much earlier. In 930 B.C. the northern tribes broke away from the temple and the Davidic kingdom and established the apostate Northern Kingdom. Counting down from the Schism of 930 B.C. to the end of the Babylonian captivity (539 B.C.) gives us almost exactly 390 years. But there is more behind the numerical symbolism. The total of 390 and 40 is 430 years (while recognizing that the periods were likely concurrent!) We read in Exodus 12:40 that the time that the sons of Israel lived in Egypt was 430 years (cf. Gal 3:17). Does the Egyptian bondage serve as the model for the 390 plus 40 years in Ezekiel's action parable? The return from the Babylonian captivity is often viewed as a "Second Exodus" in the prophets (e.g., Jer 16:14, 15; 23:7; Isa 10:26; 11:15, 16; 51:9–11).

2.5. Real Numbers with Symbolic Value

Many of the numbers in Scripture that have some symbolic significance nevertheless represent actual quantities of real entities. Whether or not the 3,000 baptized at Pentecost should remind us of the 3,000 who died at the giving of the law at Mt. Sinai, the numbers in each case represent actual individuals, allowing for customary rounding off. The Persian official Haman literally had 10 sons who were hanged (Esth 9:14). There actually were 48 (12 × 4) cities inhabited by the Levites. Job *did* live to be 140 years old (Job 42:16) even though that figure represents double the normal human lifespan (Ps 90:10) in a passage where God is increasing all that Job possessed "twofold." Both Gideon (Jerubbaal) and Ahab in fact had 70 sons who were slain in political coups (Judg 9:4–6—the assassins were hired with 70 pieces of silver; 2 Kgs 10:1, 6, 7). There actually were 70 individuals from the loins of Jacob who went down to Egypt (Exod 1:5; Gen 46:27; Deut 10:22).

The 70 elders appointed by Moses and the 70 disciples sent out by Jesus are in a slightly different category (Num 11:16; Luke 10:1, 17). These represent groups chosen by divine guidance, and the symbolic significance of "70" was likely a determination in the number chosen.

The point to be made is that a pattern of symbolic usage for specific numbers does not negate the literal reality that sometimes exists behind the numbers found. Destructive critics often choose to reject the historical reality of certain facts stated in Scripture, chalking them up to mere symbolic, figurative effect. Job's "fictitious" life, e.g., is described in the Bible as lasting 140 years simply because of the "70 × 2" symbolism. In their view there was no actual 140-year life for Job, and perhaps even no actual Job! Ahab's 70 sons are a literary concoction with no basis in historical fact, etc. As believers in the credibility of the Biblical record, however, whatever symbolic significance we find in certain numbers of individuals, animals, cities, years, etc., we must first accept the face-value statements in Scripture with regard to who did what to whom or what, when and where.

2.6. Chronological Numbers

The use of numbers that have a "qualitative" ring to them in various chronological statements in Scripture needs to be scrutinized. Numbers like "70," "400," "40," and "480" occur in chronological contexts, some narrative, others prophetic. Each instance must be evaluated with regard to the specific circumstances and possible interpretations.

2.6.1. The Number "40." To begin we would note that the reigns of the three kings of Israel's United Monarchy were 40 years each in length (Saul—Acts 13:21; 1 Sam 13:1; 2 Sam 5:5; David—1 Kgs 2:11; Solomon—1 Kgs 11:42). Although the number 40 conveys the notion of a generation-period and/or a time of testing in a number of passages, we are left with the conclusion that whatever idealistic image this 40 + 40 + 40 may seem to convey, we are primarily dealing with an actual duration of literal time for the reigns of these three monarchs.

There is one aspect of the historical situation that points to an element of idealization of symbolism with regard to these numbers, however. The numbers "40" for both Saul's and David's reign needs qualification. After Saul's death, there was a continuation of the reign of the house of Saul (Ishbosheth) over the northern tribes (Hebrew "two" years, perhaps to be read as "seven"; 2 Sam 2:10; cf. 3:1–6). David's rule over Judah was 40 years, but for the first 7 years and 6 months he ruled at Hebron *only* over Judah (2 Sam 2:11), while Ishbosheth and/or Abner were in control of the other tribes. David's 40 years then were made up of 7 1/2 + 33 (2 Sam 5:5) or simply 7 + 33 (1 Kgs 2:11). The chronology of Samuel's reign is clouded by the status of the Hebrew text at 1 Samuel 13:1, where both the numbers "forty" (years old) and "thirty" (he reigned "thirty-two" years) are absent in the Hebrew text and are supplied in some translations. It is my opinion that the missing number at both spots in 13:1 is "thirty," and that Saul was 30 years old when he began to reign (as was David later), and he reigned 32 years over Israel. (One of the possible factors in the miscopying of the text here is the frequent occurrence of words beginning with the Hebrew letter *shin*—"Saul," "years," "thirty," "two," "3,000.") If this solution be correct, then the 40 years credited to Saul in Acts 13:21 include the 7 years that his son Ishbosheth retained control over the northern tribes for the house of Saul. If so, then this same 7 year period is included in *both* Saul's and David's reign, a situation paralleled in some of the chronological summaries of later kings of Israel and Judah in which rival kingdoms or coregencies were involved.

The life of Moses can be divided up into three periods of 40 years each: 40 in Egypt (Acts 7:23—"approaching the age of forty"); 40 in Midian (Acts 7:30); and 40 in the wilderness following the Exodus (Acts 7:36). The first two enumerations are not found in the Old Testament at all, being recorded for us only in Acts 7. However, the total of 80 for the first two periods of Moses' life is given in Exodus 7:7 (and noted by the Jewish historian Josephus in his *Antiquities of the Jews* [2.15.2]). Again, the 40 + 40 + 40 represent real years, not just literary ornamentation, but it could be argued that especially the first two "40 year" periods were approximations, based on the wording of Acts 7:23.

2.6.2. The Number "400." Other chronological numbers include the number "400." In Genesis 15:13 God tells Abram that his descendants would be enslaved and oppressed 400 years (also Acts 7:6). This period is equated with "4 generations" (15:16), producing an unusual equivalency of a "generation" for "100 years" (although note that Abram was 100 when he begat Isaac). The reference to 400 years would seem to be a round number for the more precise 430 years found at Exod 12:40 (cf. Gal 3:17).

2.6.3. The Number "480." In 1 Kings 6:1 we learn that Solomon began to build the temple 480 years after the Exodus from Egypt. This is a key chronological peg for Old Testament history, and it results in a date of c. 1447 B.C. for the Exodus. This is what is known as the "early" or "traditional" date for the Exodus. A number of archaeologists and Bible scholars have argued for a later, thirteenth-century date in connection with Rameses II. This issue cannot be dealt with here, except to note the significance of the interpretation of 1 Kings 6:1 for the debate.

Those who ague for the thirteenth-century date and who wish to accept the teachings of Scripture (not all who hold this view wish to do so!) are forced to contend that the number "480" itself is symbolic, representing 12 generations (12 × 40). Since, however, a generation in reality encompasses, say, 25 years, we are left with around 300 years actual time between the Exodus (1290 B.C.?) and Solomon's temple (967 B.C.)

Several problems exist with such an approach, however. First, there is simply nothing in the text of the Old Testament to suggest such an approach. "480" does not necessarily point to "12 generations" at all. We should note that this chronological figure is not in a prophetic context, where we might expect symbolic numerical values, but in an account of Israel's past, pointing to a key foundational event in that past. It is hard to accept this number as symbolic unless overwhelming evidence demands it. In fact, however, a number of scholars have published works in recent years critical of the "late" date and supportive of the fifteenth-century dating.

A second problem for the symbolic approach to the "480" figure is that several other Biblical texts support a literal rendering in 1 Kings 6:1. We read in Judges 11:26 that Israel had already possessed the land for 300 years by the time of the Israelite judge Jephthah, at least a century and a half prior to the reign of Solomon. Another symbolic chronological reference? The figure "300" could be viewed as a "rounded number" of course, but rounded from what—130? 180? Actually the chronology for the entire period of the judges must be squeezed beyond recognition to accommodate the "late" date. The Judges reference and the natural understanding of 1 Kings 6:1 fit together perfectly.

2.6.4. The Number "70." Several periods of 70 years are described in the Old Testament within prophetic contexts. The number 70 clearly can carry a qualitative, perfective significance, but even so, a literal historical fulfillment should be investigated. Jeremiah 25:11, 12, and 29:10 refer to the duration of the Babylonian Captivity as being "70 years." It would seem that a literal approximation can be found if we begin with Judah's first deportation (Daniel and other captives) in 605 B.C. and end with the exiles' return from Babylon, 538/6 B.C., soon after the fall of Babylon in 539 B.C. We also find a second 70-year period, however, when we count from the destruction of the temple (586 B.C.) to the completion of its rebuilding (516 B.C.; Ezra 6:15). The prophet Zechariah seems to allude to this 70 year period (Zech 1:12; 7:5).

Following the fall of Babylon in 539 B.C., the prophet Daniel questions God about the promised restoration of his people (Daniel 9:2–19). The answer in a nutshell is that God has decreed a period of 70 "weeks" (of years) for the full (Messianic) restoration of Israel. The "seventy weeks of Daniel" (70 x 7 years) are a major topic of prophetic interpretation. If the decree to restore and rebuild Jerusalem (Dan 9:25) refers to the decree of Cyrus (c. 538 B.C.), then the number must be viewed as having primarily a symbolic, and not chronologically exact, characteristic. If, on the other hand, the return of Nehemiah (444 B.C.) is in mind, we are brought very close to the time of Jesus' redemptive work. The return of Ezra the scribe in 458 B.C. seems to provide the most exact chronological connection, but would seem to be the least likely candidate for fulfilling a "decree to restore and rebuild Jerusalem," at least with respect to an earthly decree. Perhaps a divine decree is intended.

But why "70 × 7"? A possible explanation can be found at the end of 2 Chronicles. In reference to the 70 year Babylonian Captivity, we read that the Jews served Nebuchadnezzar and his successors "to fulfill the word of the Lord by the mouth of Jeremiah, until the land had enjoyed its sabbaths. All the days of its desolation it kept sabbath until seventy years were complete" (2 Chron 36:21; also Lev 26:34, 35). In other words, the captivity was a time when the land could "catch up" on its "Sabbath rests." Every 7 years on the Sabbath year the land was to lie fallow. The Israelites apparently were unfaithful in their implementation of this. If a year of captivity equaled a Sabbath year missed, then the time span in question *going backwards* was "70 × 7." Taken literally, this would move us back to just before the United Monarchy began. It is possible that this idea provided the conceptual framework for Daniel's "70 weeks."

A final "70 year" period to note is that assigned to the Phoenician city of Tyre's indignation (Isa 23:15–17). Some have tried to link this to Jeremiah's 70 years regarding the Babylonian captivity, but a better approach would be to find a period within the context of the Assyrian Empire. J. A. Motyer points to the time frame between Sennacherib's invasion of Palestine in 701 B.C. and the decline of Assyria and rebirth of Tyre c. 630 B.C.[9]

The above survey of chronological numbers such as 40, 70, 400, and 480 suggests that in narrative contexts, the literal application of the

---

[9] J. A. Motyer, *The Prophecy of Isaiah: An Introduction and Commentary* (Downers Grove, IL: InterVarsity, 1993) 192–93.

number is foremost. Even in prophetic contexts, however, the literal application must be explored. When a "qualitative"/symbolic value seems present, a precise or at least an approximate literal fulfillment can often be suggested as well.

3. The Symbolic Numbers in Revelation

To an unbiased observer, the distribution of numbers in the Book of Revelation should support the view that the book is filled with figurative language and that physical fulfillments are not always to be sought. The range of the use of "7," e.g., helps us to understand that the book contains a series of cycles describing events that are not necessarily sequential, but that are in fact at times concurrent or repetitive.

3.1. The Number "7"

We find 7 seals opened (5:1–8:1), 7 angels with 7 trumpets (8:2–11:15), 7 peals of thunder (10:3), 7 angels with 7 plagues in which the wrath of God is finished (15:1), 7 golden bowls of wrath (15:7), and a scarlet beast with 7 heads (17:3). Judgment scenes conclude chapters 11, 14, 19, and 20. These are followed by a new cycle or scene depicting God's redemptive purposes. At the end of chapter 11, the seventh angel sounded (v. 15) and judgment was rendered to the righteous and the unrighteous (v. 18). This is immediately followed in chapter 12 by the scene of the woman (Israel) giving birth to Christ, and of Satan's attempts to destroy Him while on earth. Satan persecutes the woman (now the church) left behind on earth after Christ ascends to the throne of His Father (12:1–17).

The use of the number "7" characterizes the opening scenes of the book. The 7 churches of Asia (1:4), although literal, specific congregations (chs. 2, 3), clearly serve to represent God's church universal. 7 golden lamp stands represent the 7 churches, while 7 stars that Christ holds in His right hand are the "angels" (messengers/preachers?) of the 7 churches (1:16, 20). The qualitative use of "7" is evident in the designation of the Holy Spirit as "the seven Spirits who are before His throne" (1:4; we see a clear Trinitarian expression in vv. 4, 5). The 7 Spirits are later depicted as 7 lamps of fire burning before the throne (4:5). As well, the 7 Spirits of God are described as being the 7 eyes of the Lamb that are sent out into all the earth (5:6; drawing on imagery found in Zech 1:10, 11; 4:10, which in turn drew its imagery from the famous royal patrols of the Persian Empire). The Lamb standing between the 24 elders and the throne is also depicted with 7 horns (5:6).

Other symbolic numbers in Revelation, which can only be noted in passing, include "4" (4 living creatures, 4 angels at the 4 corners of the earth, 4 winds of the earth); "10 days" (2:10); "5 months" (9:5); "1/2 hour" (8:1); "1/10" (11:13); "1/3" (extensively used of destruction—8:7, 8, 10, 12; 9:15, 18); "7,000" (11:13); "12" (note later discussion); and yet others.

3.2. The Number "3 1/2"

One of the more intriguing and widespread uses of numerical imagery in Revelation involves the quantity "3 1/2." The expression found in Daniel 7:25 and 12:7 is "time, times, and half a time" in which "times" is a dual form, therefore "two times." This expression occurs at Revelation 12:14 and is parallel to the designation "1260 days," being the equivalent of 3 1/2 years of 360 days each (Rev 12:6; 11:3). This in turn is parallel with "42 months" (Rev 11:2; 13:5).

In order of occurrence the following events occur with the various designations:

1.	"time, times and a half a time" (Dan 7:25)	A "little horn" from the fourth kingdom (Rome) wears down the saints of the Highest One.
2.	"time, times, and half a time" (Dan 12:7)	The shattering of the power of the holy people is finished.
3.	"42 months" (Rev 11:2)	The holy city is trodden under foot by the nations.
4.	"1260 days" (Rev 11:3)	Two witnesses are granted authority to speak, and are slain by the "beast."
5.	"1260 days" (Rev 12:6)	The "woman" is nourished in the

		wilderness.
6.	"time, times and half a time" (Rev 12:14)	The "woman" is nourished in the wilderness away from the presence of the Serpent.
7.	"42 months" (Rev 13:5)	The "beast" is given authority to act.

Each reference above points to a period of persecution of, or opposition to, the people of God. The common time frames strongly suggest that the Serpent's attacks upon the "woman" in chapter 12 and the persecution by the "beast" in chapters 11 and 13 describe the same reality, as do the efforts of the "little horn" at Daniel 7:25. Also, a comparison of Revelation 11:2 with Luke 21:24 regarding Jerusalem's being trodden under foot during the "times of the Gentiles" seems to point to the entire church age as being involved. Of course "3 1/2" is half of "7," and seemingly indicates the opposite of the positive imagery that the latter implies. We note that when the two witnesses are killed, they are resurrected after "3 1/2 days" (Rev 11:9, 11). The 3 1/2 years/42 months/1260 days do not need to be viewed as the entire church age in an exact sense, but rather the church age viewed from the vantage point of persecution and opposition. I would suggest that the utilization of the larger number "1260," and even the "42" equivalent, helps to convey a potentially significant duration of time. If 3 1/2 years/42 months/1260 days are ways to describe the church viewed negatively, what qualitative number might describe it in a positive light?

3.3. 1,000 Years

In Revelation 20:1–6 we find reference to two positive characteristics involving the church age: Satan is bound for "1,000 years" and the saints reign with Christ for "1,000 years." Satan's power over man is greatly diminished by Christ's redemptive work (see Heb 2:14, 15, and 1 John 3:8, where Satan is rendered "powerless" and his works are "destroyed," at Christ's *first* coming). Martyrs who died at the hand of the "beast" are reigning with Christ in heaven during the church age on earth.

The cornerstone of any premillennial approach is that the "1,000 years" of Revelation 20 must be viewed as a literal duration of time. And yet, from our earlier survey of the qualitative uses of the number "1,000" throughout Scripture, along with the obvious frequency of symbolic numbers elsewhere in Revelation, there is ample reason to argue that "1,000 years" in Revelation 20 should be taken in a *qualitative,* not *quantitative* sense.

A rather intriguing argument might be made from a comparison of Revelation 20 with some of the language in the letters to the churches of Asia in chapters 2 and 3. Without going into much detail, one can show that much of the language in the letters to the churches—the tree of life, making war with a two-edged sword, ruling with a rod of iron, the book of life, walking in white robes, etc.—has parallels or counterparts in later passages in the book, especially chapters 19–22. In my mind, the content in the letter to Smyrna (2:8–11) is strikingly similar to the language found in 20:1–10, which language serves as a type of "answer" or "solution" to the situation found in the letter to the church at Symrna. Certain key phrases or ideas would seem to link 2:8–11 with 20:1–10. Note the remarkable parallels/contrasts:

	2:8–11	**20:1–10**
1.	Jesus identifies himself as the One who was dead and *has come to life* (v. 8).	Martyrs for Jesus *come to life* to reign with him (v. 4).
2.	*The devil is about to cast* (*ballô*) them *into prison* (*phulakê*, v. 10).	*The devil is cast* (*ballô*) *into* the abyss (v. 3), or *prison* (*phulakê*), (vv. 3, 7).
3.	He who overcomes will not be hurt by the *second death* (v. 11).	Those in the "first resurrection" will not suffer the *second death* (v. 6), but Satan and his followers will experience the *second death*, i.e., be *cast* (*ballô*) into the lake of fire (v. 14; 21:8).
4.	*Those faithful unto death* receive the *crown of life* (v.	*The faithful dead in Christ* come to *life* and *reign* with Christ

	10).	1,000 years (v. 4–6).
5.	*They will have tribulation "10 days" at the hands of Satan* (v. 10).	*Satan will be bound "1,000 years"* (vv. 2, 3) and *the saints will reign with Christ "1,000 years."*

Several features deserve remark. The phrase "second death" is unusual, *occurring only in these two contexts in all of Scripture.* That alone is suggestive of a link in the content of the two accounts. The imagery of the devil's casting the saints into prison is dramatically "answered" by God's casting the devil himself into "prison." Emphasis in both contexts is on the faithful dead in Christ receiving life. The intriguing point of *contrast* is the expression "10 days" opposed to "1,000 years." From the perspective of persecution, the tribulation will be a "10-day" experience, i.e., of a limited but painful nature. From the perspective of the reward, reigning with Christ will be a "1,000 year" experience. I conclude from this fascinating parallel that both "10 days" and "1,000 years" are qualitative or symbolic numbers portraying the fleeting nature of suffering for Christ in contrast to the enduring nature of reigning triumphantly with the Savior.

3.4. The Number "Two Million"

The 4 angels who are bound at the Euphrates River (whence came the ancient Assyrian and Babylonian conquerors) are released to kill 1/3 of mankind, accompanied by 200 million horsemen breathing out fire and brimstone from their mouths (9:14–18). The number 200 million seems puzzling: a huge number, but in what sense symbolic? Part of the problem again is in the translators' desire to give equivalencies. The Greek literally reads *dismyriades myriadon*, "two myriads of myriads." A "myriad" is 10,000, and represents the largest simple number in Greek, with the next largest option being "20,000," written as a single, compound word (*dismyriades*). The qualitative sense of "huge," or "unlimited" is conveyed more clearly in the Greek formulation than it is by modern English translation attempts. We find a parallel expression in Daniel 7:10 where we read, "Thousands upon thousands (lit. "a thousand thousands," Aramaic *eleph alphin*) were attending Him, and "myriads upon myriads" (lit. "ten thousand ten thousands," *ribbo ribeban*) were standing before Him. I appreciate the fact that our translators of Daniel have generally chosen not to reword this "a million" and "a hundred million." (The term *rebabah* or *ribbo*, "10,000," functions as the largest number in Hebrew and Aramaic, just as *myriades/myrioi* does in Greek). The piling up or multiplying of these "largest numbers" created the effect of being an unlimited quantity. In Revelation the translators' figure, "200 million," is huge, but quantified, and thus weakens the imagery.

3.5. The Number "666"

Of course the one number in the Bible that is clearly spelled out as symbolic is "666" (Rev 13:18). We learn that the number of the beast is the number of (a) man, "and his number is six hundred and sixty-six." The literature on this enigmatic passage is voluminous, and we can only make a few observations. The fact that Greek does not possess an indefinite article ("a, an") makes the passage ambiguous as to whether the number points to a specific individual ("of a man") or just refers to a human-based system ("of man").

In what sense is "666" the "number of man"? Since "7" is the number of perfection and deity, so it is argued, one less than that suggests imperfect humanity. Man was created on the 6th day, we are reminded, and told to labor 6 days out of the week. The ancient Sumerian, Babylonian, and Egyptian civilizations utilized a sexagesimal system (based on "60") to varying degrees. The base of the Great Pyramid is claimed to be precisely 36,000 inches (thus making the inch an ancient Egyptian reckoning). Beyond this not much can really be said. It is mildly curious that the annual tribute delivered to King Solomon was 666 talents of gold (1 Kgs 10:14), most likely just a coincidence.

Many interpreters understand the 666 symbolism to involve the Roman Empire or some specific emperor. Interestingly, adding the letters used in Latin by the Romans for numerals—I, V, X, L, C, D—produces the sum 666 (1 + 5 + 10 + 50 + 100 + 500). Irenaeus (A.D. 185) suggested that 666 referred to the pagan Roman government, based on the work *Lateinos*, "Latin (man)." Alexander Campbell (Campbell-Purcell Debate) argued that the Catholic Church is the "man of sin/beast" by using the name "the Latin Kingdom" (*hê latinê basileia*). All these examples utilize the *Gematria* principle, utilizing numerical values for the letters in various names or phrases. *The Living Bible* paraphrase at Revelation 13:18 certainly bought into this approach: "Here is a puzzle that calls for careful thought to solve it. Let those who are able, interpret this code: the numerical values of the letters in his name add to 666!" Someone has sarcastically suggested these principles: (1) If the proper name itself will not yield the sum wanted, add a title. (2) If the sum cannot be found in Greek, try Hebrew or Latin. (3) Don't be too particular about the spelling!

Commentators frequently settle on Nero as the representation/personification of anti-God world government, first-century style. The Greek form, *Neron Caesar*, when spelled in Hebrew (!) *nrwn qsr*, totals 666. The idea that Nero is being alluded to gets indirect support from a textual variant in the Greek numeration. Although "666" is the preferred reading based on the manuscript evidence, the fifth-century Ephraem Codex (C) reads "616" as did a number of other early manuscripts. These were known, but *rejected*, by Irenaeus. Bruce Metzger has observed that the change to 616 might have been intentional, based on the notion by a scribe that Nero was indeed the personage enumerated. The Latin form *Nero Caesar*, without the *n* of the Greek *Neron,* adds up to "616."[10] Armed with this new information, Del Washburn gleefully embraced the alternate reading and set out to find various "616" patterns in the Bible (*Theomatics* II), since his research on "666" patterns had not panned out very well! In my view, his "improved" results are questionable as well, with the only observation worth mentioning being that the Greek phrase "the beast" (*to thêrion*, in nominative / accusative case) has a Gematria of 616. Take that where you wish.

Modern-day candidates for "666" include Gorbachev (using the *Russian* letters for Mikhail S. Gorbachev, although one Modern Hebrew spelling option works, utilizing his full middle name Sergeevich!); Henry Kissinger (one gets to "Kissinger" with the system a = 6; b = 12; c = 18, etc.); Ronald Wilson Reagan (since his three names each have 6 letters);

---

[10] Bruce M. Metzger, *A Textual Commentary on the Greek New Testament* (New York: United Bible Societies, 1975) 750.

Bill Gates (using computer ASCII equivalents); and even Barney the Dinosaur. Of course computers (mine *is* demon possessed) and bar coding in stores have been pointed to for a while now. The new phenomenon of the Internet does give one pause, when one thinks about the wording in Revelation 13:17 regarding needing the "mark of the beast" in order to buy or sell. The ubiquitous "www" address (for "world-wide web") has as its Hebrew (and Greek) equivalent the number "666"! (I cannot resist telling about another Ronald Reagan connection. Years ago, while taking a tour of the various Beverly Hills neighborhoods, we were led by our tour guide to the gate of the Reagan property in Beverly Hills. The street address was "668." According to the guide, the original number had been "666," but Nancy made them change it when the Reagans moved there!)

Helpful hints do exist elsewhere in the Book of Revelation as we attempt to identify the designee of the "666" number. We seem to be led away from a specific individual being the beast with the description given of the harlot riding on the (scarlet) beast (17:3; cf. 13:1). Rome/ "Babylon" is being symbolized by both the "harlot" and "beast" imagery (17:1–18). At the very least, an individual/collective merging is in view with regard to the "beast." The time of the authority of the beast, 42 months (13:15) is, as noted earlier, the apparent equivalent of "time, times, and half a time" or 3 1/2 (years), and of "1260 days" (Rev 11:2, 3; 12:6, 14). *If* these qualitative time periods (denoting persecution, testing) refer to the same general situation, the conclusion would be that the "authority of the beast" went far beyond the control wielded by a single individual.

3.6. The Numbers "12,000" and "144,000"

In light of above discussions, the combination and/or multiples of "12" and "1,000" are anticipated symbolic expressions. In Revelation 7 and 14 we find 144,000 faithful ones described. We will bypass discussion of the views of the Jehovah's Witnesses and other confused interpreters of Bible prophecy. What we desire to focus on is the search for a methodology that will give us some solutions to the question of literal versus figurative language regarding such numbers.

Certainly "12" and "1,000" frequently convey symbolic significance in Scripture. Even so, we should try to look for evidence that points to the clearly symbolic nature of the "12,000/144,000" figures in the contexts in which they are found in Revelation. Such evidence is quite instructive. At Revelation 7:3–4 the 144,000 are described as bond-servants of God sealed from every tribe of the sons of Israel. The tribes from which 12,000 each were sealed are then listed. This scene then gives way to the picture of those New Testament saints ("a great multitude which no one could count") whose pure white robes had been washed in the blood of the Lamb (7:9, 14). They have come out of the "great tribulation" and are now protected and provided for by the Lamb on the throne (7:14–17).

The Old Covenant/New Covenant connection depicted here is paralleled by the scene in Revelation 12 in which the woman with a crown of 12 stars on her head gives birth to the Messiah. She is portraying here the Old Testament people of God, in my view. Yet once her man-child (Christ) is born and subsequently caught up into heaven (12:5), she then becomes the symbol of the New Testament saints, a church persecuted by the dragon and his followers (12:6–17). The woman's 12 stars offer parallel imagery to the enumeration of 12 tribes in Revelation 7.

But does the 12,000 figure for each tribe indicate a literal number of sealed/saved Old Testament believers, or is the 12,000/144,000 imagery utilizing the well-known identification of 12 with Israel and thus functioning in a qualitative and not quantitative sense? The latter is surely the case. One significant clue to the non-literalness of the tribal imagery is that the actual 12 tribes are not listed here. We know from the Old Testament that Jacob had 12 sons, including Levi and Joseph. In the later enumeration of the 12 *landed tribes*, however, these two are excluded, and replaced by Joseph's sons Ephraim and Manasseh. So which occurs here in Revelation 7—the sons of Jacob, or the tribes of Israel? The answer is *neither*. This, I believe, speaks strongly to the figurative quality of the entire description. We find Levi and Joseph included, but Ephraim and Dan excluded. The exclusion of Ephraim is striking since Manasseh is mentioned. Ephraim was the prominent tribe of the Northern Kingdom, so much so that the prophets frequently designated the Northern Kingdom as "Ephraim" (especially Hosea).

Phillip Mauro has taken the 144,000 to represent "the Israel of God" in its totality, the complete and perfect number of God's elect.[11] If he is correct, then the 144,000 standing with the Lamb in Revelation 14 represent from the perspective of the finished work of Christ the same group depicted in the Old Testament imagery in Revelation 7. The focus in chapter 14 is the fact that these individuals are holy, undefiled, faithful, purchased by the Lamb. They wear the name of the Lamb and of his Father on their foreheads, and offer a stark contrast to those who worship the beast and receive his mark on their forehead or hands (14:9–12).

It is possible, on the other hand, that the 144,000 represent a complementary group, the New Covenant Israel supplementing the Old. The imagery of the 24 elders throughout the book, apparently comprised of 12 from each dispensation, would correspond to this complementary approach. All things considered, the complete and all-encompassing nature of the 12 × 12 × 1,000 seems suggestive of the totality of the elect, viewed from different vantage points.

The description of the New Jerusalem in Revelation 21 also utilizes the 12, 12 × 12, 12 × 1,000 imagery. John describes the New Jerusalem (KJV, ASV "furlongs") in length, width, and height. The cube imagery suggests perfection and points back to the holy of holies in the Mosaic system, also a perfect cube (the notion that the dimensions of the New Jerusalem describe a pyramid is thus less likely.) The question to be answered is whether the dimensions of the city are to be taken as literal or figurative.

A more basic question is how should translators render various measurements from ancient times—with the ancient terms themselves, or with modern equivalents? I have become convinced that the ancient terms themselves should generally be used, with marginal explanatory notes as needed. This becomes especially significant when dealing in contexts that may contain figurative language involving numbers. Here at Revelation 21:16, e.g., the *New American Standard* translators made the bad decision to render "12,000 *stadia*" as "1,500 miles," a modern approximation of distance (followed, e.g., by the *New Revised Standard*

[11] Philip Mauro, *Of Things Which Soon Must Come to Pass: A Commentary on the Book of Revelation* (Grand Rapids: Eerdmans, 1933) 246.

Version). Likewise the walls of the Holy City are described in the *NASB* as "72 yards" thick (21:17), while the Greek reads "144 cubits" (a cubit being roughly 18 inches, or the distance from the elbow to the fingertips). What is obviously lost in these modern equivalents is any potential symbolism contained in the original enumerations. "12 × 1,000" has possible symbolic value, "1,500" whatever does not. "12 × 12" (144) may be qualitative, but "72" falls flat here. A *stadion* was c. 600 feet in length. If "12,000 *stadia*" were intended to convey a literal distance that could be traversed, fine. But the accompanying imagery in the immediate context of the passage suggests otherwise, and the retention of the "12,000" and "144" numerical values is essential to the interpreter's task.

Several clues exist in Revelation 21 to support the view that measurements involving "12" are representative of spiritual realities. We find 12 gates in the city walls, each described as "pearls" (v. 21) with the names of the "twelve tribes of the sons of Israel" written on them (v. 12). The wall has 12 foundation stones on which are written the "names of the twelve apostles of the Lamb" (v. 14). The city itself is described as "the bride, the wife of the Lamb" (v. 9). In one sense, the city *houses* the people of God (v. 27), but in another real sense, the city itself *represents* the people of God. God Himself is the temple (v. 22). This being the case, the 12,000/12 × 12 imagery involving the city walls seems to reinforce the concept that God's people are being portrayed, not a topographic measurement.

The final usage of the "12" imagery in Revelation adds a twist to the discussion. The Biblical account of God's dealing with man begins and ends in connection with "the tree of life." We read at Revelation 22:2, 3:

> And on either side of the river was the tree of life, bearing twelve kinds of fruit, yielding its fruit every month; and the leaves of the tree were for the healing of the nations. And there shall no longer be any curse.

In this passage we return to the cyclical imagery that the number 12 conveys. Here we find 12 kinds of fruit being provided over a "12–month" span, forever and ever. Accomplished is the sustenance and healing of the nations. The "12" imagery clearly denotes completeness with respect to provision ("twelve kinds of fruit"), duration ("every month"), and recipients ("the nations"), and fills out the symbolic cipients ("the nations"), and fills out the symbolic imagery involved with this number in describing the New Jerusalem.

4. Conclusions

The use of symbolic or qualitative numbers is an important aspect of the employment of figurative language in Scripture. Set formulas and static equations, however, must give way to careful case-by-case analysis if the numbers are really to "add up."

The following suggested guidelines serve as a summary of the present study:

1. Numerical symbolism in Scripture generally involves either numbers that represent cycles (e.g., 7, 12) or primary components in the counting system (e.g., 10, 1,000), or multiples of such numbers (e.g., 70, 12,000), or ones that point back to specific historical events or individuals (e.g., 5, 12, 430).

2. Numbers that occur in chronological contexts may involve symbolic characteristics (e.g., 70, 400), but a literal understanding should be investigated, especially in non-prophetic contexts.

3. Certain combinations of numbers (e.g., x…x + 1) occur in ancient literature as rhetorical devices, and often the literary form is more significant than the actual choice of numbers.

4. The usage of certain numbers in both Old and New Testament contexts (e.g., 3,000) may serve as an indicator of a typological connection between events.

5. The expected occurrence of certain symbolic number patterns may serve as an aid to textual criticism (e.g., "72" versus "77" in Ezra 8:35).

6. Historical facts or events that involve numbers that may possess symbolic significance (e.g., Job's age, Ahab's sons) are nevertheless *historical*, and not mere literary devices.

7. The figurative or non-figurative nature of a given context can serve to aid in the interpretation of a number or set of numbers as being symbolic or not (e.g., symbolism throughout the Book of Revelation). In turn, frequent use of clearly symbolic numbers in a given context may suggest the figurative nature of other elements in the context. (Stopping here at "7" guidelines was purely unintentional.)

It is hoped that the above treatment was an informative survey of some of the key issues involved in the understanding of symbolic numbers in Scripture. It is also hoped that the tone and content of this treatment more often evoked a smile than a groan from the one to whom it is dedicated.

CHAPTER 7

Παρουσία: A Word Study

CHARLES A. LEE

Although numerous references to the second coming are found throughout the New Testament, three words emerge as "technical terms," each of which emphasizes some significant concept of Jesus' return.[1] These three words, along with their basic thought, are as follows:

1. παρουσία (*parousia*): the presence of Christ realized fully.
2. ἐπιφάνεια (*epiphaneia*): the presence of Christ as the result of sublime manifestation of the power and love of God.
3. ἀποκάλυψις (*apokalupsis*): the revelation of the divine plan and purpose of God in its full consummation.[2]

Current interest in the second coming has again drawn attention to the need for a careful study of these technical terms to determine if they harmonize with certain points of view being expressed in popular eschatological literature. This essay will consider the term παρουσία, with particular reference to its use in 1 Thessalonians 4:15. It is in this passage that many premillennial writers find a "secret" or "silent" rapture of the church, in which millions of people will "suddenly and mysteriously" disappear from the earth.[3] Hal Lindsey, author of *The Late Great Planet Earth*, says, "In the Rapture, only the Christians see Him—it's a mys-

---

[1] George Milligan, *Saint Paul's Epistles to the Thessalonians* (London: Macmillan, 1908) 145–51.

[2] Milligan, *Thessalonians*, 151.

[3] E.g., Leon Bates, "A Tribulation Map" (Dallas: Bible Believers' Evangelistic Association, 1974).

tery, a secret. When the living believers are taken out, the world is going to be mystified."[4]

Thus, the picture derived from 1 Thessalonians 4:13–18 by many premillennialists is one in which the church, without any knowledge of the surrounding world, will suddenly and mysteriously be gone. The problem, however, is whether the technical term παρουσία is in harmony with this picture. Would the Christians in Thessalonica see such an event in their mind's eye when they read Paul's letter at this point? More specifically, what would they picture when they read the word παρουσία?

1. Morphology and Basic Meaning

The word παρουσία is an abstract noun form of πάρειμι (*pareimi*), a compound of παρά (*para*, "alongside, beside) and εἰμί (*eimi*, "to be").[5] This compound results in the idea of "being alongside" or "being present." As will be noted in the ensuing study, this thought is basic to the meaning of the word.

2. Location and Use in Scripture

2.1. Old Testament

The terms πάρειμι and παρουσία do not appear in the Old Testament in the canonical books. This is reflected in the absence of the word from the Septuagint in the books originally written in Hebrew, and "may be explained by the fact that the Semite speaks more concretely."[6]

[4] Hal Lindsey, *The Late Great Planet Earth* (Grand Rapids: Zondervan, 1970) 143.

[5] J. Stengenga, *Greek-English Analytical Concordance of the Greek-English New Testament* (Grand Rapids: Zondervan, 1963) 224.

[6] Albrecht Oepke, "παρουσία, πάρειμι," *Theological Dictionary of the New Testament* (Grand Rapids: Eerdmans, 1964) 5.859.

2.2 New Testament

In the New Testament, παρουσία occurs twenty-four times. The only gospel writer to use the term is Matthew, although John employs it in his first epistle. Arndt and Gingrich make the following distinctions in the New Testament occurrences:

1. Presence: 1 Cor 16:17; Phil 2:12; 2 Cor 10:10
2. Coming, advent, first stage in presence
   a. human beings, in the usual sense: 2 Cor 7:6, 7; Phil 1:26
   b. special technical sense: Matt 24:3; 1 Cor 15:23; 2 Thess 2:8; 2 Pet 3:4; 1 John 2:28; Matt 24:27, 37, 39; 1 Thess 4:15; James 5:7, 8; 1 Thess 3:13; 2:19; 5:23; 2 Thess 2:1; 2 Pet 1:16; 3:12
   c. as an opposing term with technical sense: 2 Thess 2:9[7]

In all of these passages there is the thought of presence or of presence being imminent by virtue of a coming or an arriving. But, as this essay will seek to establish, the arrival and consequent presence (παρουσία) of persons occupying some high rank was never a simple event. There was more meaning within the word when it applied to the arrival of a significant individual or individuals.

3. Ancient Hellenistic Usage

The classical usage denoted the simple meaning of "presence" or "arrival" of persons or things.[8] The New Testament retains this idea in such passages as 1 Cor 16:17; 2 Cor 7:6; and Phil 2:12.

As a technical term in Hellenistic Greek, παρουσία was used to refer to the visit of a ruler or high official.[9] Moulton and Milligan refer to this as the "quasi-technical force of the word."[10] This special technical

[7] Walter Bauer, Frederick W. Danker, William F. Arndt and F. Wilbur Gingrich, *A Greek-English Lexicon of the New Testament and Other Early Christian Literature* (3rd ed.; Chicago: University of Chicago Press, 2000) 780–81.

[8] William Barclay, *New Testament Words* (Philadelphia: Westminster, 1964) 222.

[9] Oepke, "παρουσία," 859.

[10] James Hope Moulton and George Milligan, *The Vocabulary of the Greek Testament* (London: Hodder and Stoughton, 1930) 497. Milligan observes, "*Parousia*, as ap-

use is underscored by the elaborate preparations which accompanied the arrival. "For the visit of Ptolemy Soter to the village of Cerceosiris 80 artabae of corn have to be collected."[11] Oepke states in this regard:

> The customary honours on the *parousia* of a ruler are: flattering addresses,...tributes,...delicacies, asses to ride on and for baggage, improvement of streets,...golden wreaths *in natura* or money, and other honours had to be paid for by the population of the district favoured by the *parousia* of the king or his ministers, and if voluntary gifts were not enough a forced levy was made, which led to much complaint.[12]

A papyrus from the third century B.C. mentions contributions made for a crown (στέφανος [*stephanos*]) for presentation to the king at his "arrival" (παρουσία), and a letter written from one Appenneus in 264 or 227 speaks of making preparation for the visit (παρουσία) of Chrysippus, "...by laying in a number of birds for his consumption."[13]

Sophocles, in the fifth century B.C., uses παρουσία in verse one of his *Electra* to refer to an "occasion."[14] This usage is closely associated with that of the arrival of a dignitary and does not substantially change the thought. παρουσία also referred in Hellenistic Greek to the helpful coming of the gods, but in a narrower sense, such as in a healing experience.[15] Consequently, there is some indication that the term tended to combine a sense of the presence of deity by the revelation of divine

plied to the Return of the Lord, is simply the Anglicizing of a Greek word (παρουσία) which literally means 'presence.' But in late Greek the word had come to be applied in a quasi-technical sense to the 'visit' of a king or great man. Thus in a papyrus of the third century B.C. we read of a district that was mulcted to provide a 'crown' for one of the Ptolemaic kings on the occasion of his 'visit'" (*Here and There Among the Papyri* [London: Hodder and Stoughton, 1922] 75–76).

[11] Barclay, *Words*, 223.

[12] Oepke, "παρουσία," 860.

[13] Moulton and Milligan, *Vocabulary*, 497.

[14] Henry G. Liddell and Robert Scott, *A Greek-English Lexicon* (Oxford: Clarendon Press, 1940) 1343.

[15] Oepke, "παρουσία," 864.

power with the official visit of a person of high rank.[16] Such a combination is well suited to the New Testament usage of the term when referring to the coming of a divine king.

4. New Testament Times

The use of the Septuagint in New Testament times does not appear to have formulated any special meaning for παρουσία in the New Testament writers. In the Septuagint the term is limited to those works originally composed in Greek, and then only in a profane sense.[17]

> But the very occurrence of the word is significant. Hellenistic Judaism took it from its environment. That it also found its way into religious usage may be seen from *Testaments of the Twelve Patriarchs* [2nd-1st century B.C.].... The technical sense does not seem to have been normative at first. But one may assume that it soon exerted an influence.[18]

The word παρουσία does not occur in Philo, but Josephus uses it to refer to the Shekinah and combines παρουσία with δύναμις (*dunamis*) in his *Antiquities* (9.55).[19] Although it can be shown that Judaistic and Christian eschatology are closely allied, the religious uses of παρουσία in Judaistic literature are channeled through Hellenistic meanings as they relate to the New Testament application of the term.[20] Thus it would appear that παρουσία in Paul, Matthew, James, John and Peter is related somewhat more closely to the then-current, popular idea of the coming of a dignitary. Such usage was still quite common, as is attested in the contemporary ostraca.[21]

---

[16] Bauer, Danker, Arndt and Gingrich, *Lexicon*, 781.

[17] Oepke, "παρουσία," 864.

[18] Oepke, "παρουσία," 864.

[19] Oepke, "παρουσία," 864; Gingrich and Danker, *Lexicon*, 630.

[20] Burton S. Easton, "Parousia," *International Standard Bible Encyclopedia* (Wilmington, DE: Associated Publishers and Authors, 1915) 4.2249.

[21] Moulton and Milligan, *Vocabulary*, 497.

παρουσία refers as well to the coming of the Antichrist in the last times (2 Thess 2:9) and even here retains the idea of the revelation of a supernatural power in conjunction with the appearance of a significant person ("according to the work of Satan"). This was certainly not intended to convey the idea of a happy occasion in the minds of the Thessalonians, but the παρουσία of kings and conquerors was not always met with great popular acceptance:

> *Parousia* is sometimes used of the "invasion" of a province by a general. It is also used of the invasion of Asia by Mithradates. It describes the entrance on the scene of a new and conquering power.[22]

Such a scene would presumably be analogous to the triumphant march of the German army through Paris and down the Avenue Foch on June 14, 1940. The pomp and the people were there but the popular acceptance was not.

5. Grammatical Considerations

No significant understanding of the term in the New Testament is derived from grammatical or idiomatic considerations, except that "Paul always uses παρουσία with the genitive."[23] No stress is given to the word with the use of periphrasis or idiom by New Testament writers, which suggests strongly that παρουσία painted its own picture quite clearly. As Wuest says, "The Christians of the first century felt the parallelism between the *parousia* of the reigning emperor and the *parousia* of Christ."[24]

---

[22] Barclay, *Words*, 223–24.

[23] Oepke, "παρουσία," 868.

[24] Kenneth S. Wuest, *Bypaths in the Greek New Testament* (Grand Rapids: Eerdmans, 1940) 34.

6. Ecclesiastical Period

From the early history of the church there was a strong belief in the return of Christ, although the word παρουσία does not occur in Acts.[25] As a technical eschatological term, it is found in the *Epistle to Diognetus* (c. A.D. 117) and the *Shepherd of Hermas* (c. A.D. 140).[26] Later church fathers continue to use παρουσία, but the evidence of specific "trappings"—such as careful preparation, public celebration and pomp—do not seem regularly to attend the word. In the *Gospel of Nicodemus* (second century A.D.) and Justin's *Apologies* (c. A.D. 150), the expression is simply ἡ δευτέρα παρουσία.[27] In Justin's *Dialogue with Trypho the Jew* (c. A.D. 150), the apologist speaks of ἡ ἔνδοξος παρουσία τοῦ Χριστοῦ (*hê endoxos parousia tou Christou*, "the esteemed *parousia* of Christ"), an expression which apparently retains an element of the New Testament idea.[28] Even though it appears that the New Testament meaning began to fade in the post-apostolic era, there is evidence that Christians of the sixth century were still quite conscious of the technical force of the word.[29]

Eventually παρουσία took on a two-fold meaning in post-apostolic writers, including both the incarnation and the second coming.[30] Indeed, considerable use is made of the term by the early fathers to refer exclusively to the first advent.[31] Milligan makes the following analysis:

> It would seem, therefore, that as distinguished from other words associated with Christ's Coming, such as His "manifestation"

---

[25] Oepke, "παρουσία," 867.

[26] Oepke, "παρουσία," 870.

[27] Joseph H. Thayer, *A Greek-English Lexicon of the New Testament* (New York: American Book Company, 1889) 490.

[28] E. A. Sophocles, *Greek Lexicon of the Roman and Byzantine Periods* (Cambridge, MA: Harvard University Press, 1914) 861.

[29] Moulton and Milligan, *Vocabulary*, 497.

[30] Oepke, "παρουσία," 870–71.

[31] Sophocles, *Lexicon*, 861.

(ἐπιφάνεια) of the Divine power and His "revelation" (ἀποκάλυψις) of the Divine plan, the "parousia" leads us rather to think of his "royal visit" to His people, whether we think of the First Coming at the Incarnation, or of the Final Coming as Judge.[32]

7. Conclusions

The technical term παρουσία in the New Testament connotes several significant ideas that produce a picture in the reader's mind. The "presence" of someone or something is generally indicated by the word. When referring to someone who is not physically present, it conveys both impending arrival and consequent presence. When the subject is a significant person or persons (royalty, aristocracy, etc.), παρουσία picks up certain trappings such as public celebration, pomp, and widespread change in the usual lifestyle of the community.

The use of παρουσία in 1 Thessalonians 4:15 does not permit the interpretation of a "secret" or even "quiet" arrival of Jesus Christ, the Divine King. Indeed, the entire "rapture passage" (1 Thess 4:13–18) is one of the noisiest sections in the entire Bible.[33] It would appear therefore from this study of the word παρουσία that the secret rapture doctrine of current popular eschatological literature is in error.

Certain questions which cannot be considered in this paper need further study with regard to the eschatological technical terms of the New Testament. More needs to be explored , for example, relative to the absence of παρουσία in the Septuagint. As was noted above, Oepke suggests that the explanation for this may lie in the more concrete vocabulary of the Hebrew that underlies the Septuagint. This word was extremely common, however, and the existence of a gap between its total absence in the Septuagint and a significantly increased use in the New

[32] Milligan, *Papyri*, 76.

[33] An interesting story is told by George Murray in *Millennial Studies: A Search for Truth* (Grand Rapids: Baker, 1948) 137–38: Dr. Rowland Bingham, when asked by his wife where he found the secret rapture in the Scripture, pointed her to 1 Thess 4:13–18. She remarked that this was "about the noisiest thing in my Bible." The ensuing investigation greatly altered Dr. Bingham's eschatological position.

Testament is puzzling.[34] The terms ἐπιφάνεια and ἀποκάλυψις need careful study with reference to the current eschatological doctrines as well. The position taken by many premillennialists is that these terms parallel certain distinctions between a pre- or post-tribulation rapture and the second coming.[35]

There is a conspicuous correlation between the cultural setting of the church and its emphasis on the second coming. As the persecutions of Rome subsided, deliverance and imprecatory eschatology tended to fade. During the expansion of western democracy, which created a generally optimistic milieu, the postmillennial doctrine prevailed.[36] In our time, faced with the decadence of western culture and the potential rise of an anti-Christian world order, the preoccupation with a dispensational premillennial eschatology has overwhelmed the evangelical community. Whether motivated by vindictive aspirations for a world ruled by the Messiah, or the hope for an escape from the inevitable tribulations of the people of God, millions of people now support this view.

This essay has attempted to provide an insight into New Testament eschatology by exploring the connotations of one of three technical terms. It is hoped that a single word's meaning might help to focus more on the importance of grammatical-historical exegesis in the area of Biblical eschatology and generate less reliance on the waxing and waning of cultures, political powers, and economic systems.

---

[34] A. T. Robertson, *A Grammar of the Greek New Testament in Light of Historical Research* (Nashville: Broadman, 1934) 81.

[35] J. Dwight Pentecost, *Things to Come* (Grand Rapids: Zondervan, 1958) 156–58.

[36] William T. Moore, *A Comprehensive History of the Disciples of Christ* (New York: Revell, 1909) 19–37.

CHAPTER 8

The Temple in the Gospel of John

BRIAN JOHNSON

> The Temple was, in Jesus' day, the central symbol of Judaism, the location of Israel's most characteristic praxis, the topic of some of her most vital stories, the answer to her deepest questions, the subject of some of her most beautiful songs. And it was the place Jesus chose for his most dramatic public action. It has long been recognized that the evangelists were alive to the symbolic value of Jerusalem, Mount Zion, and the Temple itself—so much so, in fact, that they were able to weave it as a theme into their writings in a fairly sophisticated manner. It would be very strange if Jesus himself were not equally aware of the significance of the place described by the psalmist as "the joy of the whole earth."[1]

1. Introduction

If the evangelists "wove" the theme of the temple into their Gospels, as the above quote by N. T. Wright suggests, how is this theme presented in the Gospel of John? In this article I will attempt to detect this theme and to understand how the author presents the temple. Further, I will argue that understanding the temple theme in the Gospel of John gives good insight into John's purpose in writing his Gospel. In the analysis below, it can be seen that John carefully and intentionally used this theme within his Gospel.

During the period leading up to and inclusive of the first century A.D., the temple was a central feature within Judaism. "The Temple was considered to be the very dwelling place of God, in a way shared by no

---

[1] N. T. Wright, *Jesus and the Victory of God* (Minneapolis: Fortress Press, 1996) 406.

other place on earth."[2] This does not mean that groups within Judaism always (or even often) agreed on the proper use of the temple and its place in worship. That the temple so often served as a point of conflict between such groups, only serves as further illustration of its importance. As E. P. Sanders has stated, "I think that it is almost impossible to make too much of the Temple in first-century Jewish Palestine."[3]

The destruction of the temple in A.D. 70 marked an end to the temple's sacrificial system and in some ways made these issues moot. However, this also marked the beginning of a new debate regarding the proper response to the destruction of the temple. How does one worship now that the temple is gone? Stephen Motyer in a recent book-length study has argued that the Gospel of John was written precisely to answer this question within a post-destruction-of-Jerusalem setting.[4] Even if one does not accept Motyer's thesis, the very fact that he *can* make such an argument shows that the temple plays an important role within this Gospel. Furthermore the Gospel of John does seem to provide an alternative to the temple and its worship in the person of Jesus.

In this study I have attempted to consider every passage in the Gospel of John where the temple is mentioned explicitly, either through the terms ἱερόν (*hieron*) or ναός [*naos*], or where the temple is referred to by a descriptive word of phrase. What I have not included in this study, however, are passages where the temple is not mentioned but might be inferred from the context. Perhaps the best example of this is that I have not attempted to treat every account of the Jewish feast. However, the feast of tabernacles in chapter 7, where the temple is mentioned explicitly as the setting and where the subject matter is directly pertinent to the temple, I have included.

---

[2] M. O. Wise, "Temple," in *Dictionary of Jesus and the Gospels* (eds. Joel B. Green, Scot McKnight, and I. Howard Marshall; Downer's Grove, IL: InterVarsity Press, 1992) 813.

[3] E. P. Sanders, *The Historical Figure of Jesus* (London: Penguin Books, 1993) 262, as quoted in Wright, *Victory*, 406, n. 127.

[4] Stephen Motyer, *"Your Father the Devil"?: A New Approach to John and "the Jews"* (Paternoster Biblical and Theological Studies; Carlisle: Paternoster Press, 1997).

2. Passages Dealing with the Temple

There are two basic types of references to the temple in John. First, the temple sometimes occurs as a backdrop to the action taking place. These references will be saved for consideration in point 2.4 below. The second type of reference to the temple in John would be teaching or action that directly involves the temple. These will be considered in the order in which the occur in the narrative, beginning with the "temple incident" recorded in John 2.

2.1. The Temple Incident (John 2:13–22)

The first explicit mention of the temple in the Gospel of John is an important one.[5] In John 2:13–22, John recounts the temple incident.[6] It is important for two reasons. First, there are indications that its placement has been carefully chosen. Understanding why the author has placed it where he has is crucial for our understanding of the temple in the Gospel as a whole. Secondly, this first appearance of the temple sets out connections which alert the reader to uses of the temple further along in the Gospel. In some ways it almost serves as a "thesis statement" regarding the temple and its relationship to Jesus. Therefore, I will first consider the placement of the temple incident and attempt to understand the significance of what this incident tells us about the temple.

2.1.1. John's Placement of the Temple Incident. It is first important to notice where John places the temple incident. This placement becomes significant when it is compared with the Synoptic Gospels. While the Synoptics recount a temple incident just prior to Jesus' death, John places the incident very early in his narrative, and *apparently* at least, very early in the ministry of Jesus. It might be suggested that it is ille-

[5] There is perhaps implicit reference to the temple in 1:14, 'The Word became flesh and made his dwelling (ἐσκήνωσεν [*eskênôsen*]) among us. We have seen his glory (δόξαν [*doxan*])…" See R. J. McKelvey, *The New Temple: The Church in the New Testament* (Oxford Theological Monographs; London: Oxford University Press, 1968) 75. While this is possible, it does not fit the criteria I have explained above for inclusion in this article.

[6] Because of the debate over how Jesus' action in the temple is to be understood, I have chosen the phrase "temple incident" in an attempt to remain neutral on this point.

gitimate to make a case for John's placement of the temple incident through comparison to the Synoptics. However, there are some indication within the Gospel of John to suggest that its readers would have been familiar with the broad outlines of the life of Jesus as it is presented in the Synoptics, if not familiar with one or more Synoptics complete.[7] Without going into great detail into this debate, perhaps it would be sufficient to point to two passages. First, John the Baptist's testimony in 1:29–36 seems to assume prior knowledge of Jesus' baptism. Secondly, in order for the irony of John 7:42 to be appreciated, the reader would have to be familiar with Bethlehem as Jesus' place of birth. Therefore, if the reader was familiar with Jesus' action in the temple at the end of his ministry, as the Synoptic tradition places it, his or her attention would be drawn to John's placement of the temple incident toward the beginning of his narrative.

I have left open the question of whether there were one or two temple incidents in Jesus' life. Some scholars have suggested that there were two temple incidents: one early in Jesus' ministry which is recorded by John and one leading up to Jesus' arrest and crucifixion as recorded by the Synoptics authors.[8] Others have argued for one such incident which either John moved to an earlier point in Jesus' ministry or which the Synoptic authors moved to connect with his death. Without arguing for one interpretation over the other, I would simply point out that either shows the importance of John's placement of the incident. Whether John is moving the temple incident to an earlier point in the narrative or choosing to recount the earlier of two (or more) incidents in Jesus' life, I would argue that he is intentionally making a point regarding how the temple is to be understood in relation to the story of Jesus' life.

Even if it is not accepted that the readers were aware of the Synoptic tradition of the chronology of Jesus' life, there is an indication within the text itself that its placement should be understood as significant by the

---

[7] For example note Richard Bauckham's recent argument that the Gospel of John was intended for a readership which knew Mark ("John for Readers of Mark," in *The Gospels for All Christians: Rethinking the Gospel Audiences* (ed. *idem*; Grand Rapids: Eerdmans, 1997] 147–71).

[8] For example Craig Blomberg, *The Historical Reliability of the Gospels* (Downer's Grove, IL: Inter-Varsity Press, 1987) 170–173.

reader. The author closes this pericope with an anachronistic statement which pushes ahead the "narrative time" to the end of the story.[9] In v. 22 John writes, "After he was raised from the dead, his disciples recalled what he had said. Then they believed the Scripture and the words that Jesus had spoken." If the reader was not previously aware of how the story of Jesus' life ends, he or she is now! The literary critic Gérard Genette has called an intentional anachronism of this type a *prolepsis*.[10] That the author interjects this *prolepsis* shows that he wants the reader to understand that this account will have a later significance.

2.1.2. The Importance of the Temple Incident. If, indeed, John's choice of recounting the temple incident at this place in the narrative tells us he is presenting this as a theme, what does his recounting of the incident itself tell us about how he understands this theme? It will be seen in what follows that in several ways this account sets the tone for the passages dealing with the temple later in the Gospel.

First it is obvious that there is a strong element of conflict within this passage. Jesus' reaction to the sellers and money-changers is dramatic, but there is also an element of conflict in the Jews' reaction to him. Second the connection made between this incident and Jesus' death is important. The Scripture from Psalm 69 which the disciples recalled in relation to Jesus' action point toward Jesus being consumed. Jesus' statement to the Jews "destroy this temple" when interpreted with the knowledge that he was speaking of "the temple of his body" also points toward Jesus' death. Thirdly, the parenthetic statement that Jesus was speaking of the temple of his body is itself crucial. Jesus is in the temple itself during this account, and the discussion with the "Jews" is understood by them to be centered upon the physical temple building itself. The narrator gives us indication that the reader is required to radically reinterpret the "temple."

---

[9] See particularly the discussion of this in Derek Tovey, *Narrative Art and Act in the Fourth Gospel* (Journal for the Study of the New Testament Supplement Series 151; Sheffield: Sheffield Academic Press, 1997) 229–255.

[10] Gérard. Genette, *Narrative Discourse: An Essay in Method* (trans. Jane E. Levin; Ithaca, NY: Cornell University Press, 1980) 40.

How could Jesus' body be the temple? In other ways John presents Jesus' ministry as a fulfillment of Judaism. This has been perhaps best noted in relation to John's use of the feasts. In a similar fashion John states strongly here that Jesus is to be understood as a fulfillment of the temple. The center of worship is moved from the location of the temple to the *person* of Jesus. As we consider other passages below, it will be clear that this is not simply a "one-off" statement, but is an important element of the entire theme of the temple in this Gospel. Much of the Gospel hinges upon the identity of Jesus. It is significant that at this early point and in such an explicit way Jesus is identified with the temple.

2.2. The Samaritan Woman (John 4:1–26)

In chapter 4 John relates a meeting which took place between Jesus and a Samaritan woman. Although the temple is not the central point of this pericope, Jesus' response to a statement by the woman gives further information on how the temple is to be understood. When the woman begins to believe in Jesus as a "prophet," she is immediately drawn to a major point of separation between the Samaritans and the Jews—the proper place of worship (v. 20). The Samaritans thought Mt. Gerizim was the proper place of worship rather than the temple in Jerusalem. For a period of time a temple had even stood on Gerizim, and even though it had been destroyed in 128 B.C., Samaritans continued to worship there.[11] Jesus' answer however, is that neither the Samaritans' place of worship, nor the Jewish place of worship are to be the proper place of worship in "the time" which "is coming." Instead Jesus makes the declaration that the worshipers will properly worship "in Spirit and in truth." The emphasis upon proper worship in this passage adds another element to our understanding of the way the temple is presented in the Gospel of John. In this eschatological statement, Jesus is not advocating another place of worship as opposed to the Jewish or Samaritan places of worship. Instead he is announcing that there is a time coming when the focus of worship will no longer be upon a "place." As Brown states, "Jesus is speaking of

[11] George R. Beasley-Murray, *John* (Word Biblical Commentary 36; Dallas: Word, 1987) 61.

the eschatological replacement of temporal institutions like the Temple, resuming the theme of" the temple incident.[12]

Within this context, of course, this is significant because the first distinction between Jew and Samaritan which the woman fixes upon, according to Jesus will not be an issue at all. Lines of separation based upon places of worship will not be properly maintained in the Kingdom. If the major emphasis of this passage is on the universal nature of Jesus' message, then we can see how this fits into the context. For the purposes of understanding the theme of the temple in this Gospel, this passage is important because the reader is again being pointed toward a reinterpretation of the temple and even of what it will mean to worship God properly. Worship is no longer to be tied to a location.

Perhaps it would be fitting to make one further point here. Neither the word ἱερόν (*hieron*) nor ναός (*naos*) normally translated as "temple" is included in this passage. However it seems clear enough that when the place (ὁ τόπος [*ho topos*]) of worship in Jerusalem is mentioned, the Jerusalem temple is what would be in the mind of a first-century person. In fact, given the proper context, one possible definition of τόπος (*topos*) is "temple."[13] I mention this not only to defend my inclusion of this passage in this study, but also because this is not the last time we find such a use in the Gospel of John.

2.3. The Feast of Tabernacles (John 7:14–52)

The use of the feasts within the Gospel of John is an important study in its own right. As Motyer has noted, both the temple and the feasts form an important theme in this Gospel. He writes, "Not only is the cleansing of the Temple given a prominent position at the head of the

---

[12] Raymond Brown, *The Gospel According to John* (Anchor Bible 29; Garden City, NY: Doubleday, 1966) 180.

[13] Walter Bauer, Frederick W. Danker, William F. Arndt and F. Wilbur Gingrich, *A Greek-English Lexicon of the New Testament and Other Early Christian Literature* (3rd ed.; Chicago: University of Chicago Press, 2000) 1011. Note definition 1b, but see also 1a. This is clearly the way Brown understands τόπος here: "it refers to the Temple," (*Gospel According to John*, 172). See also Günter Haufe, "τόπος" in *Exegetical Dictionary of the New Testament*, (ed. Horst Balz and Gerhard Schneider; Grand Rapids: Eerdmans, 1993) 3.366.

narrative, but the festivals are closely woven into the structure of the Gospel."[14] It is obvious that the feasts will be closely linked with the theme of the temple. However, I have singled out this occasion recorded in John 7 for closer consideration because it mentions the temple explicitly but also because the pericope deals with the theme of the temple directly. Because Solomon's temple was dedicated at the Feast of Tabernacles (1 Kings 8:2) "this gave the feast a special relation to the Temple."[15]

Jesus' activity and teaching here are directly connected to the Feast of Tabernacles. This is particularly true of Jesus' action on the greatest day of the feast. Central to understanding this passage is understanding John 7:37–38. Jesus' statement here can be understood in two completely different ways depending upon how it is punctuated. The text of the NIV illustrates the way these verses are most often understood: "If anyone is thirsty, let him come to me and drink. Whoever believes in me, as the Scripture has said, streams of living water will flow from within him." Translated in this way the one from whom the living water flows is the one believing in Jesus. This is the traditional understanding and one which is widely supported.[16]

However, there is another possibility which must be consider in light of both the immediate context and the context of the Gospel as a whole. The marginal note in the NIV suggests the alternate translation of Jesus' statement, "If anyone is thirsty, let him come to me. And let him drink, who believes in me. As the Scripture has said, streams of living water will flow from within him." This is often called the Christological interpretation of these verse because in this case the one from whom the living water flows is Jesus. There are several reasons for preferring this translation. But I will mention only two.[17] First, it fits with Jesus' claim

---

[14] Motyer, *Your Father the Devil*, 36.

[15] Brown, *Gospel According to John*, 326.

[16] See Gary M. Burge, *The Anointed Community: The Holy Spirit in the Johannine Tradition* (Grand Rapids: Eerdmans, 1987) 88, n. 162, for a list of scholars and translations favoring this understanding.

[17] For a complete defense of the Christological interpretation see Burge, *Anointed Community*, 88–93, along with the scholars he lists who agree with this interpretation, n. 164.

to be the source of living water in John 4:10. Second, John 7:39 identifies this water with the Spirit. In the Gospel of John Jesus is consistently seen as the giver of the Spirit.

If Jesus' statement is understood in this way, it is very appropriate given the context of the Feast of Tabernacles. Central to the celebration of Tabernacles was prayers for rain along with a symbolic act. On each of the seven days of Tabernacles the priest would fill a golden pitcher with water and march to the altar in front of the temple where he would pour the water into a silver funnel and onto the ground.[18] Therefore Jesus' claim to be the source of living water against this background becomes even more striking. But, what makes it significant in our discussion of the temple? For this, we must also consider the OT background against which these actions were set.

In Zechariah 9–14 the Feast of Tabernacles is connected with an eschatological "day of the Lord." An earthquake is depicted which splits the Mount of Olives "in two from east to west, forming a great valley." (v. 4) Other cataclysmic events accompanying the coming of the Lord are described, including the description, "On that day living water will flow out from Jerusalem, half to the eastern sea and half to the western sea, in summer and winter" (v. 8). After a description of a plague which will strike Jerusalem's enemies, it is said:

> Then the survivors from all the nations that have attacked Jerusalem will go up year after year to worship the King, the Lord Almighty, and to celebrate the Feast of Tabernacles. If any of the peoples of the earth do not go up to Jerusalem to worship the King, the Lord Almighty, they will have no rain. (vv. 16–17)

The provision of water seems to be central to how Tabernacles was understood and celebrated by the time of the first century. The source of the water which would nourish all nations is certainly Jerusalem and likely the temple. This passage is often read in conjunction with Ezekiel 47. This follows an injunction in Ezekiel 45–46 to keep the feasts and new moons. A description here is given of water flowing "from under the threshold of the temple toward the east...and the water was flowing from

[18] Brown, *Gospel According to John*, 327.

the south side" (vv. 1, 2). This water becomes a river which is described as life giving both to fruit trees lining its banks and even allowing fish to live in the Dead Sea (vv. 8–12). Here it is clear that this life-giving water flows from the temple itself.

When this background to Jesus' statement in John 7:37–38 is considered, the significance for our present study can be seen. Jesus shouts at the Feast of Tabernacles that *he* can provide "living water." This must be understood as Jesus claiming that he will fulfill the prophecies of Zechariah 14 and Ezekiel 47 both of which might have been in the people's minds. The crowd certainly understands these claims as Messianic. As McKelvey stated,

> "Jesus' claim to supply living water could not fail to challenge Jewish readers. It meant that the centre and source of the world's life was no longer the temple of Jerusalem, but himself, the new temple."[19]

This passage, like the temple incident in John 2, points to a later fulfillment. Following Jesus' statement the author inserts another prolepsis. "By this he meant the Spirit, whom those who believed in him were later to receive. Up to that time the Spirit had not been given, since Jesus had not yet been glorified" (John 7:39). As Jesus' body is identified as the temple in chapter 2, here in chapter 7 the Holy Spirit is identified as the life-giving water which was promised in connection with tabernacles and which Jesus promises to provide.

So in this account Jesus is again shown to be the one who is able to provide what the temple was expected to provide. We find in this account elements of conflict such as were present in the account of the temple incident. Here the people question why the authorities are allowing Jesus to speak publicly (vv. 25–26). The reaction of the chief priests and Pharisees was to attempt to arrest Jesus (v. 32). This attempt was foiled apparently because of the way Jesus' teaching influenced the guards who had been sent. When confronted by the chief priests and Pharisees about why they had not succeeded, the temple guards reply, "No one ever spoke the way this man does" (v. 46). This provokes fur-

---

[19] McKelvey, *New Temple*, 81.

ther outrage (vs. 47–49). Here the source of the conflict is not Jesus' statement regarding the temple as much as it is that Jesus is speaking publicly *in* the temple courts.

Some of the teaching which Jesus does in the temple courts is to show his close relationship with the Father. He is sent from the Father and Jesus also *knows* the Father. He makes clear that this is a unique relationship by stating "you do not know him" (vv. 28–29). Also Jesus says that he is going back to the one who sent him, but they cannot come to where he will be (vv. 33–34). One further point is that much of the later part of this account deals with Jesus' identity. In particular some say he is "the Prophet" or the "Christ," while others say he cannot be because of he is from Galilee. If forced to summarize the message of the Gospel of John in one brief statement, it would not be far wrong, I think, to answer "the identity of Jesus." Certainly the author states his purpose in 20:31 in prompting belief in his readers that "Jesus is the Christ, the Son of God." So it is to be expected that Jesus' identity as the Christ would be a central question in these passage. We also find, however, questions about the relation of the Christ to the temple.

As I stated at the beginning of this section, the feasts in the Gospel of John deserve attention in their own right. Because of the close connection between the feasts and the temple within Judaism, is it perhaps artificial to suggest that one be examined closely without examining the other just as closely? In isolating the thread of the temple as it is woven into the fabric of the Gospel, however, it is not my purpose to try to tease that thread out and therefore unravel the garment. Nevertheless, I would suggest that in concentrating on the temple alone we might better see how it functions within the Gospel and so understand the whole Gospel better as a result. As we follow our thread we will perhaps see how it joins with other threads and how they together are skillfully woven to make up the fabric of this Gospel.

2.4. Temple as Background

As mentioned earlier sometimes the temple seems to serve only as a backdrop for the actions and teaching of Jesus. However, even where the temple's presence seems incidental there are indications of uniform thought as regards the temple. In this point I will present five passages where the temple serves either as background or is mentioned incidentally. This is primarily for the sake of completeness in looking at all of the explicit statements regarding the temple; however, it is possible that these passages will add to our overall understanding of the theme of the temple.

2.4.1. The Healing of the Lame Man (John 5:1–15). It is possible that the temple is more than background in this passage, though it is only explicitly mentioned in v. 14. The geographical details in this passage are often pointed to in order to show the author's awareness of the layout of Jerusalem before the destruction by the Romans. What is pursued less often is the question of whether the author is making a point by including such specific references to where this event took place. Do we have an example of the evangelist weaving his theme "in a sophisticated manner" here? I would say that possibly we do.

The location where this healing miracle of Jesus takes place is a pool "by the Sheep Gate." This gate was very close to the temple on the northern side. Further it was apparently connected to the temple because of its use, being the gate through which sacrificial animals could be easily brought—thus its name. It has been suggested that this scene setting is intentional with Jesus in the shadow of the temple providing something that the temple and its system of worship could not provide. One greater than the temple is here (Matt 12:6).

There is conflict here with the Jews, but it is primarily centered on Jesus healing on the Sabbath. There is, of course, a specific mention of the temple in this passage as the place where Jesus found the man. Here in the temple Jesus enjoins the man to "stop sinning or something worse may happen to you." It is interesting that here Jesus takes the authority upon himself to speak on matters of sin. Beasley-Murray is surely right that rather than understanding Jesus' statement as connecting the man's being crippled with sin, Jesus should be understood as commenting on the man's salvation.[20] "Jesus carries out the work of God in deliverance from sin and death for life eternal."[21]

---

[20] It might be significant that immediately following Jesus' statement the man left the temple.

[21] Beasley-Murray, *John*, 74.

2.4.2. Controversy with the Pharisees (8:12–30). In 8:12–30 there is an account of conflict between the Pharisees and Jesus. In verse 20 there is an almost incidental comment, "He spoke these words while teaching in the temple area near the place where the offerings were put. Yet no one seized him because his time had not yet come." Certainly this comment about the temple has most to do with verifying the public nature of the encounter. However it is interesting to notice the similar themes connected with this location which we have seen previously. There is the conflict here with a group within Judaism—this time the Pharisees. Also, in what comes after verse 20, Jesus speaks of his death in connection with salvation. "Once more Jesus said to them, 'I am going away, and you will look for me, and you will die in your sin.'" Additionally, in verse 28 Jesus speaks of the "Son of Man" being lifted up and of the close connection between himself and the Father. These are clear throughout the Gospel of John and so perhaps it is coincidental that the temple is mentioned here in connection with them. After all, much of the action in John's Gospel takes place in Jerusalem and so it is natural that the temple should be seen in these contexts.

2.4.3. Jesus Greater than Abraham (8:48–59). Toward the end of chapter 8 Jesus makes further claims about himself, this time in connection with Abraham. In verse 59 when the Jews prepare to stone Jesus we are told that he "hid himself, slipping away from the temple grounds." This is another incidental mention of the temple as background for the event. Again, however, this is in a context of conflict.

2.4.4. The Feast of Dedication (10:22–42). In chapter 10 at the Feast of Dedication Jesus is seen to be walking in an area of the temple known as Solomon's Colonnade. Here he is confronted by the Jews and told that if he is the Christ, he should say so plainly. In the discussion that ensues, Jesus again speaks of the closeness between himself and God, saying in verse 30, "I and the Father are one." Again the reaction of the Jews is to pick up stones to stone Jesus. So again the temple serves as the scene of conflict with the Jews over Jesus' teaching.

2.4.5. Jesus before Annas (18:23). The final incidental mention of the temple is a statement of Jesus as he is on trial before the high priest in John 18. It is different than the others in that the temple is not the background of the narrative. Jesus is questioned about what he has taught, to which he replies in v. 20, "I have spoken openly to the world….I always taught in synagogues or at the temple where all the Jews come together. I said nothing in secret."

2.4.6. Summary of incidental statements. It would be wise to be careful with these statements. In every case the temple is not the main point of the passage which we have considered. Jerusalem in general and the temple in particular are where much of the action in the Gospel of John takes place. The emphasis upon feasts in this Gospel, particularly the emphasis upon the Passover, draws the reader's attention quite naturally to the temple where elements of these feasts take place. However, when this thread it highlighted, we cannot help but notice the themes we find arising again and again. Most notable would be the theme of conflict. In light of not just these passages but the ones we have considered previously, it would not be an overstatement to say that in the Gospel of John the temple is a point of heated conflict between Jesus and "the Jews."[22]

2.5. Meeting of the Sanhedrin (John 11:45–57)

In this passage the conflict between Jesus and the Jewish leaders can be seen to assume a fevered intensity. After Lazarus' being raised from the dead, many put their faith in Jesus, but others went to the Sanhedrin prompting a meeting. This passage recounts the events of that meeting. There are several indicators that a new level of resolve has been reached by the leaders which will ultimately and unavoidably result in Jesus' death. The high priest Caiaphas states the inevitable necessity of Jesus' death. Verse 53 states, "So from that day on they plotted to take his life." We find that they ordered for anyone who knew Jesus' whereabouts to report it to them. (v. 57) The result of this is that Jesus "no longer moved about publicly among the Jews." All of this seems to imply that the next

[22] The identity of "the Jews" is not a central point of this article. However, because of the frequency of the use of this description, it is an important issue within the study of the Gospel of John. It would perhaps be wise to note that often, as regards the theme of the temple in John's Gospel at least, the conflict is often between Jesus and a leading group within Judaism, the Pharisees or chief priests for example. See J. A. Weatherly, "Anti-Semitism" in *Dictionary of Jesus and the Gospels*, 13–17, esp. point 2.1.2. See also Motyer, *Your Father the Devil*, 54–57.

appearance which Jesus makes in Jerusalem will result in his death. This sense of expectancy is increased with the musing of the people "in the temple area" as the Passover approaches: "Isn't he coming to the Feast at all?" (v. 56). This whole passage has the element of an approaching "showdown."

There is a sense of irony in the use of the temple in this passage, however. The reason the Sanhedrin gives for needing to stop Jesus is their fear that "the Romans will come and take away both our place and our nation" (ἡμῶν καὶ τὸν τόπον καὶ τὸ ἔθνος [*hêmôn kai ton topon kai to ethnos*], v. 48). As was noted when discussing the Samaritan woman, τόπος can refer to the temple. While τόπος in this verse could possibly be understood as referring to Jerusalem, there is a good parallel in 2 Macc 5:19 where τόπος occurs in conjunction with ἔθνος and refers to the temple.[23] The irony here is that the Sanhedrin's solution to keep their temple from being taken away, the death of Jesus, has been shown throughout the Gospel to this point to be the very act which will see the significance of the temple superseded by Jesus! Now it is admittedly difficult to determine if the author intended this connection to be made, but what is *certain* is that the author makes a point of showing the theological significance of Caiaphas' statement about Jesus' death. According to John, in his office of high priest Caiaphas prophesied "that Jesus would die for the Jewish nation, and not only for that nation but also for the scattered children of God, to bring them together and make them one." (vv. 51–52) In his death and what he accomplishes by it, Jesus gathers together not only the remnant but all nations to himself.

2.6. Summary of the Temple Theme in the Gospel of John

At this point it might be well to stop and survey where we have journeyed thus far. In examining the explicit references to the temple within the Gospel of John we have seen several points of similarity in these accounts. First, the temple is often connected with Jesus' death. Craig Evans in an article on the temple incident writes:

---

[23] See Brown, *Gospel According to John*, 439. Also Bauer, Danker, Arndt and Gingrich, *Lexicon*, 1011, though they do not come down strongly for either definition 1a or 1b in this instance.

> A temple motif of sorts is present in John, though it is not the same as that in Mark. Whereas in Mark the emphasis is on Jesus' opposition to the temple, in John it is the reverse. Every mention of the temple in John is in the context of Jesus being threatened with death (2:14–22; 5:14–18; 7:14–20; 8:59), arrest (8:20; 11:56–57), or both (10:22–39; 18:20 [Jesus has been arrested and placed on trial]).[24]

Second, there is teaching about proper worship. This is surely to be expected as the temple served as the center of Jewish worship. This is perhaps best seen in the discussion between Jesus and the Samaritan woman. Third, Jesus' identity is often a subject in these passages and particularly the close identification between the Father and the Son. Fourth, there is in almost every case we have considered an element of conflict.

I have argued that John placed the account of Jesus' action in the temple at the beginning of his narrative intentionally and that he drew attention to it by connecting this event with Jesus' death and also by stating that the temple is properly interpreted as Jesus' body. This interpretation continues to be important beyond the confines of this one pericope as Jesus is consistently shown to be taking upon himself roles normally ascribed to the temple. John's presentation of the temple hinges on this relationship to the person of Jesus.

Herbert Giesbrecht in an article dealing with this point in relation to the Gospel of John's ecclesiology summarized thus:

> But that Jesus was also endeavoring to suggest something of the deeper truth that the Jewish Temple was only a foreshadowing of the temple of his own body and of the coming church which he would establish through his death and resurrection, is clearly intimated by the wider context. Jesus' enigmatic response to the brusque questioning of the Jews concerning his authority to commit such an outrageous act, when it is studied in the light of other pertinent passages in this Gospel (as, for instance, Jesus' authoritative

[24] Craig Evans, "Jesus Action in the Temple," *Catholic Biblical Quarterly* 51 (1989) 243, n. 17.

> and unparalleled teaching in the precincts of the Temple Court—7:14–32; 10:22–39; and 18:20–21—and his remarks to the Samaritan women in Sychar about a time "when true worshippers will worship the Father in spirit and truth"—4:21–24), gradually evokes a deeper level of significance: here is a teacher of Israel who, more truly than any other, possesses both the authority and the qualifications to become Israel's true Leader and Ruler in respect to all aspects of their spiritual life, both now and in the future.[25]

If we have correctly interpreted the theme of the temple in the Gospel of John and if we have emphasized its importance correctly, what might be expected is a climactic conclusion to this theme. This is present with other Johannine themes such as Jesus as the lamb of God. Early in the Gospel (John 1:29, 36) Jesus is declared to be "the Lamb of God who takes away the sin of the world." This theme and its relation to Jesus' authority to forgive and the emphatic importance of the Passover is developed throughout the Gospel. The death of Jesus, then, occurs as the Passover lambs are slaughtered, and is confirmed when it is found not necessary to break Jesus' legs fulfilling the Scripture "not one of his bones will be broken," (John 19:36) which probably refers to the requirement of Exodus 12:46 that the Passover lamb's bones were not to be broken.[26] With other themes John has proven himself to be able to skillfully use the Scriptures and practices of Judaism to make his argument that Jesus is the Christ and the fulfillment of Jewish worship. Is it possible that he does the same with the theme we have interested ourselves in? I would argue that in fact it is possible that he has done so in one section of the Farewell Discourse of Jesus.

3. The Temple in John 14:1–3

While the beginning of John 14 is among the best-loved passages in Christianity, it is not among the easiest to understand. In addition to

---

[25]Herbert Giesbrecht, "The Evangelist John's Conception of the Church as Delineated in his Gospel," *Evangelical Quarterly* 58 (1986) 108.

[26] Stephen S. Smalley, *John: Evangelist and Interpreter* (2nd ed.; Carlisle: Paternoster Press, 1998) 254.

some translation difficulties, it is perhaps the fact of how well-loved these verses are which makes them difficult to understand. That they are often pulled out from the context and read on their own makes it essential that they be understood within the context. These words of Jesus do bring comfort, and I would never suggest that it is wrong to recite them in times of trial. However to do so *exclusively* might cause us to miss the place of this passage within the Gospel as a whole. To understand them is to make firm the basis for the comfort they provide.

The purpose of this section is not to provide a detailed exegesis of 14:1–3 but to make suggestions regarding the way these *could* be understood. I will argue in this section that this passage could be understood as a drawing together of the theme of the temple in the Gospel of John. In fact, these verses might provide the climactic conclusion to this theme. This passage is not normally understood as referring to the temple at all, but I will argue there is good reason to do so. If this proves to be an adequate understanding and to have explanatory power then it would be useful to do a detailed exegesis of this passage from this point of view. First, I will consider how a careful reader of the late first century might have understood this passage when first encountering it. This will provide some justification for pursuing this line of thought. Secondly I will suggest how this passage might be understood in light of what we have seen already presented by the author of the Gospel of John regarding the temple.

In chapter 13 Jesus has given his disciples some difficult news. He is going to be betrayed by one of their number. Then, to the beloved disciple, at least, this betrayer is identified as Judas. Jesus then begins to speak of his death and chapter 13 ends with the revelation that Peter will deny Jesus. In 14:1 Jesus then gives words of comfort to his disciples, exhorting them to trust both in God and himself. What becomes significant for our purposes in understanding this passage is how a first-century reader would understand the next phrase: "In my Father's house are many μοναί (*monai*)." μοναί (translated in the NIV as "rooms") has been notorious difficult to translate. I will consider possibilities below. However, before this I would draw attention to the phrase "the house of my Father" (ἐν τῇ οἰκίᾳ τοῦ πατρός μου [*en tê(i) oikia(i) tou patros mou*]). I would suggest that this phrase would have been full of meaning to the first-century reader and can be easily identified, especially within the context of the Gospel.

When reading the Gospel of John straight through, one is first struck by the fact that similar phrases occurred twice before, both in chapter 2 in the account of the temple incident.[27] In 2:16 Jesus says, "How dare you turn my Father's house (τὸν οἶκον τοῦ πατρός μου [*ton oikon tou patros mou*]) into a market!" This is echoed in the disciples' remembered quotation of Psalm 69:9: "Zeal for your house (τοῦ οἴκου σου) will consume me." It is obvious in chapter 2 that the referent of "my Father's house" is the temple. It is possible, and in fact likely, that the same referent would be called to mind with Jesus' words in chapter 14.

It is worth drawing attention to the fact that two different Greek words lay behind the translation "house" in these two passages. Some might be tempted to argue that Jesus does not say the same thing at all in chapters 2 and 14 because οἶκος is used in chapter 2 while οἰκία is used in chapter 14. However, in this period these two words really do not represent vast differences in meaning. By the Hellenistic period any distinction had disappeared so that in the New Testament οἶκος and οἰκία are synonymous.[28] John himself uses both terms in other contexts. In 7:53 (per the variant in some manuscripts) and 11:20 he uses οἶκος, while he uses οἰκία in 4:53, 8:35, 11:31, 12:3. Even if some slight distinction remains, Leon Morris has thoroughly pointed out that the use of close synonyms interchangeably is an aspect of Johannine style.[29]

The Psalm 69 quotation of the disciples gives another important clue that "my Father's house" would have been naturally understood as a refer to "temple." "House" was used often in the OT to refer to the temple of YHWH as well as the temples of other gods. In his article on *naos*, for instance, von Meding writes, "The OT refers much more often to the temple by means of the simple Heb. term *bayit* (Gk. *oikos*) house, than

---

[27] From our perspective perhaps the fact that these are the only two places in all of Scripture where "my father's house" occurs would be considered significant.

[28] J. Goetzmann, "οἶκος," *New International Dictionary of New Testament Theology* (ed. Colin Brown; Grand Rapids: Zondervan, 1976) 2.247.

[29] Leon Morris, "Variation—A Feature of the Johannine Style," in *Studies in the Fourth Gospel* (Grand Rapids: Eerdmans, 1969) 293–319.

by using the Sumerian-derived word *hekal* (Gk. *naos*), temple."[30] "My Father's house" is not used elsewhere in Scripture; however, in Matthew 12:4 (and the parallels Mark 2:26 and Luke 6:4) "the house of God" is used to refer to the temple.[31] "House," of course, could simply refer to a place to live, but the indication that a place of worship was intended is when it was coupled with the deity's name.[32] In the Gospel of John "Father" is the title most frequently used by Jesus to refer to God.[33] So if *oikos* is associated here with God through the use of Jesus' title "Father," then the simplest way of understand "my Father's house" in this context is as a reference to the temple.

Additionally, we have seen that "place" (τόπος [*topos*]) can also be used to refer to the temple and is used in this way twice in the Gospel of John (4:20; 11:48). Twice in this passage we have τόπος being used. Jesus says, "I am going there to prepare a place for you. And if I go and prepare a place for you, I will come back and take you to be with me that you also may be where I am." By themselves it would be improper to argue that these should be understood as references to the temple. However, because of the context where it seems that Jesus is referring to the temple by the use of "my Father's house," the use of these terms to refer to a "place of worship" is possible.

It should be noted that not many understand a reference to the temple in John 14:1–3.[34] "Father's house" is normally either taken immedi-

---

[30] M. von Meding, "ναός," *New International Dictionary of New Testament Theology*, 3.782.

[31] "House of God" occurs in three more NT passages: 1 Tim 3:15, Heb 10:21, and 1 Pet 4:17.

[32] J. Goetzmann, "οἶκος," 247.

[33] Larry Hurtado, "God," *Dictionary of Jesus and the Gospels*, 274–275.

[34] To list a few commentators who do not: Bultmann, Brown, Carson, Ashton, Ridderbos (Burge, *Anointed Community*, 145; Leon Morris, *The Gospel According to John* [New International New Testament Commentary; Grand Rapids: Eerdmans, 1971] 638). Hermann N. Ridderbos writes, "'House' as a term for the place where God resides conveys an idea found frequently in both the Old Testament and in Jewish and Hellenistic writings of the time of Jesus. But in these writings 'house of God' is normally used of the temple, not heaven. In any case, the focus of the expression here is that it is 'my Father's'

ately to refer to heaven or it is taken in some sense as a corporate reality as we see similar phrases used in other NT writings.[35] However, when taken within the context of the discussion that ensues it should be seen that this explanation is at least possible. Thomas' question which immediately follows this passage shows that he understands Jesus to be speaking of a location while Jesus' answer focuses upon his identity. (vv. 5–7) This certainly fits with the Johannine presentation of the temple theme as we have seen. The center of worship is being transformed from the location of the temple to the person of Jesus. The discussion of Jesus' relation to the Father leads to Philip's request for the Father to be shown to them (v. 8). In Jesus' answer again he stresses the close relation between himself and the Father. Even as the temple has been the means by which to draw near to God, now Jesus has taken on that role.

Understanding this passage in this way can perhaps help to make clearer at least one difficult question in this passage. That is, as was alluded to earlier, the difficulty of the meaning of μονή [*monê*] in verse 2.[36] Part of the difficulty lies in the fact that there are only two occurrences of this word in the NT and both are in this chapter (John 14:2, 23). This difficulty has not been made easier by a quirk of the English language. The translators of the Latin Vulgate rendered μονή as *mansio* which means "a halting place."[37] Therefore, the translation of μονή in the KJV and the ASV is "mansion."[38] To complicate the matter even

house, the place where Jesus goes because he is at home there" (*The Gospel according to John: A Theological Commentary*, [Grand Rapids: Eerdmans, 1997] 489–90).

[35] See Beasley-Murray, *John*, 249–250.

[36] This was first pointed out to me by Professor Thomas Friskney, to whom this article is humbly dedicated. While it was my parents who first taught me a passion for God's Word, it was Professor Friskney who taught me the proper expression of that passion in the form of careful and detailed study for the purpose of adequately communicating God's message to others. For that I offer him my profound thanks.

[37] See Raymond Brown, *Gospel According to John*, 618–619, on whom much of the rest of the paragraph is dependent. See also Robert H. Gundry, '"In My Father's House Are Many μοναί [Monai]" (John 14:2)' *Zeitschrift für die Neuentestamentliche Wissenschaft* 58 (1967) 68–72; and Beasley-Murray, *John*, 249.

[38] As in the KJV and ASV.

further, these were probably influenced by Tyndale's translation, but in Old English mansion simply meant "dwelling place" (as opposed to "halting place") and had none of the connotations of large buildings with huge columns in front with which the word is often connected today!

So what does μονή mean? A grand home? Certainly any place connected to God will be grand and the connotations of Jesus' statement that there are "*many* μοναί" in his Father's house is that it is expansive. That is to say, no one is going to be left out. However, the word μονή itself does not denote what we would normally attach to the idea of "mansion" today. As was explained above, it is an accident of language that these ideas were ever connected in the first place. Should we understand μοναί as "stopping places" or "resting places" as seems to be implied by the Vulgate and has been argued by others? Perhaps, but this might not be the best understanding of the word. So what about "dwelling places" as the NIV translates? This is perhaps the best understanding, but with the proper emphasis upon dwelling.

While μονή is used only twice in the Gospel of John it is closely related to word which is used frequently in John: μένω (*menô*, "to remain or abide"). Robert Gundry, in a short but perceptive article, points out that μένω in the Johannine literature often "denotes present spiritual relationships" and that in the immediate context of John 14–15 abiding is a *leitmotif* or key theme.[39] Therefore, he states, "Could it be clearer from context that the first thing we are to think of when reading, "In my Father's house are many μοναί," is not mansions in the sky, but spiritual positions in Christ, much as in Pauline theology?"[40] I think that Gundry has made an excellent point here. However, he goes on to then interpret "my Father's house" as a "household or family."[41] I would suggest that Gundry's explanation of μοναί works even better with an understanding of "my Father's house" as the temple reinterpreted as Jesus. Again dwelling spiritually in Jesus allows the believer the access to God which had been formerly afforded by the temple. Through his death Jesus be-

[39] Gundry, "In My Father's House," 70

[40] Gundry, "In My Father's House," 70.

[41] Gundry, "In My Father's House," 70–71.

comes the "new temple" and provides all that goes with it. He provides forgiveness of sins. He provides the salvation which will be made available to all. Perhaps most important in the immediate context, he provides a way to the Father. Even as the temple in Jerusalem provided the place where God dwelt, now access is direct as there is a mutually reciprocal dwelling between God, Jesus, and the believer.

4. Conclusion

I have argued within this article that John intentionally develops the theme of the relationship between Jesus and the temple by arguing that Jesus supersedes the temple. I would agree with the assessment, "For John's community Jesus' body is the Temple that has replaced the Temple of former times."[42] What the temple had provided in the past now is provided in the person of Jesus. As Wright states, "For Jesus, part of the point of the kingdom he was claiming to inaugurate would be that it would bring with it all that the Temple offered, thereby replacing, and making redundant, Israel's greatest symbol."[43] In his death Jesus becomes the Lamb of God. He becomes the sacrifice which takes away sin, thus making temple sacrifice redundant. Furthermore, as the Son he enjoys a uniquely close relationship with the Father and he becomes the means by which his disciples can draw close to God. It is no longer necessary for the temple to provide and mediate contact between God and his people. Jesus has taken on that role as well. As Jesus takes on these roles the temple is made redundant and the focus of worship shifts from the location of the temple to the person of Jesus. The believer properly worships through Jesus. It is possible as well that John 14:1–3 should be understood as a climax to this theme. While I believe this theme is evident in the Gospel of John, to the careful reader it is perhaps expressed best and more clearly in a passage from another Johannine writing. In the description of the new Jerusalem comes the descriptive detail, "I did not see a temple in the city because the Lord God Almighty and the Lamb are its temple" (Rev 21:22).

---

[42] W. R. Herzog II, "Temple Cleansing," *Dictionary of Jesus and the Gospels*, 820. Note here that I would understand John's community to be John's intended readership.

[43] Wright, *Victory*, 435.

CHAPTER 9

Restoring the Kingdom

DENNIS GAERTNER

The Book of Acts begins with a familiar scene. Before his ascension Jesus is speaking with his disciples. For forty days after the crucifixion and resurrection he has appeared to them, showing himself alive and speaking to them "about the kingdom of God" (Acts 1:3). Now during a meal he instructs them directly to remain in Jerusalem because the Father is ready to send the gift that has been promised—the gift that includes their baptism with the Holy Spirit.

But when the Lord mentions the outpouring of the Holy Spirit, it leads the disciples on a later occasion at the Mount of Olives to pose another question. Was Jesus at this time "going to restore the kingdom to Israel" (1:6)? Jesus' response deals with the issue of time. They should not expect to know "the times or dates" since the Father has set these "by his own authority." Instead Jesus delivers a promise and a commission. The disciples would receive "power when the Holy Spirit" came on them and they would be witnesses for Jesus "in Jerusalem, and in all Judea and Samaria, and to the ends of the earth" (1:8).

Several issues have been raised by commentators dealing with this episode. Does Acts contain this exchange between Jesus and the disciples as a way of dealing with the delay of the parousia?[1] What did the disciples mean by referring to the restoration of Israel?[2] Why did the dis-

---

[1] Hans Conzelmann argued this position in his *The Theology of St. Luke* (trans. Geoffrey Buswell; London: Farber & Farber, 1960).

[2] The Greek verb ἀποκαθιστάνω (*apokathistanô*, "restore") can be understood as an eschatological technical term describing God's ultimate restoration of Israel in the end time. See Fritz Rienecker, *A Linguistic Key to the Greek New Testament* (trans. Cleon Rogers, Jr.; Grand Rapids: Zondervan, 1980) 263.

cussion of the outpouring of the Spirit raise this question in their minds?[3] What connection does Acts imply between the ascension of Jesus and the restoration of Israel?[4]

But a further question which has recently been raised is to what extent was Jesus' reply to their question a rebuke or a correction? In an article entitled "Did Jesus Correct the Disciples' View of the Kingdom?" John McLean concludes that commentators who see in Jesus' response to the disciples' question any redefinition of the kingdom are mistaken. He points to Acts commentators like Gerd Lüdemann, Ernst Haenchen, Simon Kistemaker, F. F. Bruce, Charles Carter and Ralph Earle as examples of those who maintain that Jesus was describing a spiritual kingdom in contrast to the disciples who were looking for a national, political entity.[5]

McLean argues that these commentators have misunderstood the dialogue between Jesus and his disciples in Acts 1:6–8. Jesus, he says, "did not redefine the kingdom by mandating the proclamation of the gospel." Instead, Jesus' reply affirms "the disciples' belief in the restoration of the kingdom to Israel." His reply is not a rebuke or a correction. When the disciples voiced expectations about the restoration of Israel as a political entity, Jesus' objection was not to their concept of the nature of the kingdom, but only to their speculations about the timing of its establishment.[6]

His conclusion in this article includes a call to imitate the faith of the disciples in Acts 1:6. If the disciples "conceived of a future national kingdom for ethnic Israel in which they will reign with Christ," then why

---

[3] Commentators frequently call attention to the association in Jewish thinking of the outpouring of the Spirit and the end of time. See John Polhill, *Acts* (The New American Commentary; Nashville: Broadman, 1992) 84.

[4] David Tiede sees in Acts all of the elements of the "restoration of Israel" unfolding one by one, beginning with the exaltation of Christ at the ascension, and including the preaching of repentance, the division in Israel, and the expanding mission to the Gentiles. See his "The Exaltation of Jesus and the Restoration of Israel in Acts 1," *Harvard Theological Review* 79 (1986) 278–86.

[5] John Mclean, "Did Jesus Correct the Disciples' View of the Kingdom," *Bibliotheca Sacra* 151 (1994) 215–27.

[6] McLean, "Did Jesus Correct," 218–19.

should modern believers reject this expectation. Believers, he says, "should anticipate not only the second coming of Jesus Christ, but also His establishment of a future kingdom for the nation of Israel."[7]

Similarly, Anthony Buzzard expresses unhappiness at commentators on Acts 1:6. Why explain the disciples' question as "utterly out of tune with their Lord's teaching" as if they were "tragically inadequate" in their understanding of "Christianity's central theme" of the kingdom? He adds to the list William Barclay, H.A.W. Meyer, John Calvin, Albert Barnes, John Bright, George Ladd and *The Pulpit Commentary*.[8] Buzzard points out that no clear contradiction of their concept of the kingdom is seen in these verses, even though Luke is quite free to record the "slowness of the apostles to grasp truth" on other occasions, as he does for example in Luke 18:34 when he records that the apostles were slow to understand that the Messiah had to die.[9] He quotes Hans Conzelmann with approval when he makes the point, "Acts 1:6 speaks of the Kingdom being restored to Israel. It is not the hope of this which is rejected, but only the attempt to calculate when it will happen."[10]

Thus Acts 1:6 is taken as an indication that the eschatological hope which resounds in the Book of Acts is one that "is fully in line with the Davidic Messianism presented by Hebrew prophecy" in terms of a national restoration of Israel.[11]

Buzzard argues strenuously that the promise of a restored Israel is not fulfilled in the crucifixion and resurrection of Jesus; that even the songs of Mary and Zechariah at the birth of Jesus are prophetic words which point to accomplishments of Jesus which will come after the Parousia.[12] The Book of Acts, he insists, acknowledges no fulfillment of this promise. Rather, it is because of a "disastrous theory of over-realized

---

[7] McLean, "Did Jesus Correct," 227.

[8] Anthony Buzzard, "Acts 1:6 and the Eclipse of the Biblical Kingdom," *Evangelical Quarterly* 66 (1994) 197–215.

[9] Buzzard, "Eclipse of the Biblical Kingdom," 202–03.

[10] Conzelmann, *Theology of St. Luke*, 163.

[11] Buzzard, "Eclipse of the Biblical Kingdom," 203.

[12] Buzzard, "Eclipse of the Biblical Kingdom," 205.

eschatology" that modern Christians have misinterpreted the restoration of Israel as fulfilled in the resurrection and ascension of Jesus.[13] In so doing, the Jewish context of this promise has been set aside because the kingdom of God has been redefined "as 'heaven' for departed souls or a synonym for the church or a social program, or even Zionist hopes this side of the Parousia."[14]

For this reason, Buzzard urges commentators to "adopt the mindset of the apostles for a moment" and allow themselves "the liberty of supposing that these disciples of Jesus in fact knew exactly what they were talking about."[15] Thus he concludes that "a new orientation to biblical eschatology is needed" and proposes that Acts 1:6 should be a starting point.[16]

The conclusions of McLean and Buzzard offer some important cautions to those who take seriously the words of Jesus in Acts 1:6–8. It is certainly possible to overspiritualize Jesus' teaching of the kingdom of God. It is true that Jesus' response to the disciples focuses on their speculation about times and dates and it is also true that Jesus' reaction to the disciples leaves the kingdom as something yet to come—something evidently not completely fulfilled in the crucifixion and resurrection of Jesus. Similarly, it is true that Jesus' words may be understood as not overturning the disciples' expectations of a restored Israel, though he does stop short of endorsing their concept of the nature of this kingdom.

The observations of McLean and Buzzard do, however, seem inadequate as arguments for a more literal interpretation of Jesus' teaching about the kingdom of God. Their "either/or" approach to these issues leaves room for much more consideration of the nature of this kingdom. Having rejected an interpretation which makes the crucifixion and the resurrection of Jesus the fulfillment of the promise of the kingdom, they assume that the only alternative is a political, national entity which comes at the return of Christ. This approach fails to reckon adequately

---

[13] Buzzard, "Eclipse of the Biblical Kingdom," 209.

[14] Buzzard, "Eclipse of the Biblical Kingdom," 210.

[15] Buzzard, "Eclipse of the Biblical Kingdom," 212.

[16] Buzzard, "Eclipse of the Biblical Kingdom," 213.

with the message which presents itself prominently in the Book of Acts—the mission to the Gentiles as part of the "restoration of Israel."

To admit that the apostles were using a term expressing Jewish expectations of a political restoration is easy enough since the verb ἀποκαθιστάνω (*apokathistanô*, "restore") readily lends itself to such an interpretation.[17] Similarly the Gospel of Matthew presents Jesus' words about the restoration of all things (17:11) as an expectation of future events involving Elijah. To say that no spiritualizing may take place regarding the theme of restoring all things, however, ignores the fact that Jesus' words are understood by Matthew to refer not to a literal return of Elijah, but to the ministry of John the Baptist. In other words, in the preaching of John the Baptist the way was being prepared for the restoration of all things.

Regarding the question of Acts 1:6 it must also be noted how closely related are all the statements in 1:6–8.[18] The disciples ask the question about the restoration of Israel in 1:6, a question which is followed by Jesus' correction regarding dates and times in 1:7. Then comes what seems to be further elaboration in terms of a broader answer to their question about the restoration of Israel in 1:8. Remembering this structure of the exchange between Jesus and his disciples helps the reader to grasp the new focus Jesus brings to the disciples' concept of the restoration. Jesus does not reject their view, but he certainly broadens it. The restoration will begin as these apostles receive power from the Spirit to become witnesses for Christ "in Jerusalem, and in all Judea and Samaria, and to the ends of the earth." Thus the restoration of Israel will begin with Jews, but then reach far into the Gentile world.

This is precisely the story of Acts. Had Christ wanted to, he could have opted for other, more political, directions. As F. F. Bruce points out, Josephus documents several Jewish movements in the first century which seemed motivated by an attempt at a political restoration of Israel.[19] Ju-

---

[17] See the discussion of Jewish Messianic expectations in George Foot Moore, *Judaism in the First Centuries of the Christian Era* (Harvard, 1927; reprint Peabody, MA: Hendrickson, 1997) 2.323–76, where the restoration of a "Golden Age" is prominent.

[18] Polhill, *Acts*, 84.

[19] F. F. Bruce, *The Time Is Fulfilled: Five Aspects of the Fulfillment of the Old Testament in the New* (Grand Rapids: Eerdmans, 1978) 15–19.

das the Galilean determined that the time for God to restore Israel had arrived, and perhaps using the Old Testament Book of Daniel as his inspiration, led a revolt against Rome to establish a Jewish kingdom that would supplant Gentile dominion. The Romans crushed the revolt. Even the Jewish War which began in A.D. 66, according to both Roman and Jewish authorities, found its inspiration in Old Testament prophecies which were taken to mean a political restoration of Israel.[20]

Note how carefully Jesus avoids such a concept in Acts 1:6–8. It is not enough merely to say that Jesus did not rebuke the apostles for a nationalistic application of the hope of restoration, but it is essential that Jesus' response, especially in 1:8, be taken seriously. The restoration of Israel was coming, but it would involve spiritual issues of salvation, for the Gentiles as well as the Jews. It was a lesson that even John the Baptist had to learn. When he sent messengers to Jesus asking whether Jesus was the Coming One, or if they should look for someone else, Jesus told the messengers to consider the activities of his ministry—that the "blind receive their sight, the lame walk, lepers are cleansed, and the deaf hear, the dead are raised up, the poor have good news preached to them"(Luke 7:22). As Bruce points out,

> By such teaching, together with the active ministry which accompanied it, Jesus showed the character of the kingdom which he proclaimed…the consummated kingdom would bear the same character as the kingdom which was even now breaking in.[21]

If John saw in Jesus' ministry a fulfillment of Messianic expectations, then he also should have seen a corrective to his view of the kingdom as one which is political and national. He should have seen a kingdom more like what Jesus envisioned in 1:8.

Thus Acts begins with an invitation to the reader. Listen to the apostles as they ask about one of the most important eschatological questions of the day, and then watch how Jesus responds, pointing to their future mission as the answer to their question. Next, watch how that mission is carried out. Jacob Jervell has drawn attention to the way Acts

---

[20] Bruce, *The Time Is Fulfilled*, 17.

[21] Bruce, *The Time Is Fulfilled*, 23.

emphasizes that "the promises fulfilled in Christ belong to Israel and that a share in these promises is given to the Gentiles."[22] The phrase "to the Jew first and then to the Gentile" describes the progression of gospel preaching and acceptance in Acts. "Israel" continues to refer to the Jewish people, including both those who repent (that is, become Christians) and those who resist the gospel. Luke does not paint a picture of a Jewish nation which wholly rejects Christ. Those Jews who accept Christ are counted as "the purified, restored, and true Israel."[23]

Supporting this contention are the mass conversions of Jews recorded in Acts.[24] In connection with Jewish conversions, Luke is much more inclined to cite numbers. In 2:41 there are 3,000 converted; in 4:4 the number is 5,000; in 5:14 still more are added; in 8:6 the number increases dramatically; and then the epitome is reached in 21:20 where tens of thousands of Jews are included in the number. Acts also tells the story of Gentile converts, but his concern to show that Israel is responsive to the gospel is obvious.

As is so often true in the New Testament, Acts shows how future hopes are beginning to be fulfilled in the present. Jesus Christ came as Messiah, but was rejected by those who should have received him gladly. He was crucified and rose on the third day, ascending to the Father where he waits for the final restoration (Acts 3:21). The process of restoring Israel, however, has already begun in Acts, as Jews are converted to Christ, and Gentiles are brought into the kingdom to share in the blessings which originally belonged to the Jews. The day will come when Je-

---

[22] Jacob Jervell, *Luke and the People of God: A New Look at Luke-Acts* (Minneapolis: Augsburg, 1979) 42.

[23] Jervell, *Luke and the People of God*, 43.

[24] See 2:41, 47; 4:4; 5:14; 6:1, 7; 9:42; 12:24; 13:43; 14:1; 17:10ff.

sus will return, and only then will it become clear to what extent Christ's presence is "a time of refreshing" for both Jews and Gentiles (3:19).

CHAPTER 10

Conjugating Christianity: A Sermon on Hebrews 3:1–4:11

STEVE HOOKS

I had the great privilege of serving with Tom Friskney on the faculty of Cincinnati Bible College and Seminary for twelve years. During that time my appreciation for him grew to admiration. A rare blend of academician and churchman, of great thinker and humble servant, he personified the gentleman scholar. I shall ever be in his debt not just for what he taught me about the Scriptures, but what he taught me about the One of whom they speak.

A devoted preacher, Tom always enjoyed a sermon "tied closely to the word." I offer this meager attempt of such homily in honor of his outstanding career and even more outstanding life.

Introduction

Christianity is not a "noun." It is a "verb." It is about what God has done, is doing and shall do. It is about what we were, are and shall be. Christianity believes, it hopes, it loves. Christianity cares, it serves, it gives. It is more than an institution. It is an action, a state of being.

Our "predicate" of faith can be conjugated in at least three tenses:

Christianity is a religion of the past tense: an "old-time religion" of what was and has been. It is about tradition and precedent, remembering and rehearsing the mighty deeds of God.

It is a religion of the future tense: a "by-and-by" religion of what shall be. It is about prediction and fulfillment, awaiting and anticipating the promises of God.

But, most importantly, it is a religion of the present tense, a "here-and-now" religion of what is. It is about conviction and conduct, believing and behaving in response to God's call.

In the text before us the author explores the three tenses of Christianity in what amounts to a call to spiritual renewal. Three times he quotes from Psalm 95:7—"Today, if you hear his voice, do not harden your hearts"—in an effort to motivate the church to live for "today," in light of the lessons of the past and the promises of the future.

The author begins his summons to spiritual renewal by taking these Hebrew Christians on a painful trip down memory lane, urging them to:

Learn from the Past

The writer of Hebrews takes the readers back to that infamous time in the wilderness when their forefathers rejected God's call to enter Canaan. In 3:8 he warns, "Do not harden your hearts as you did in the rebellion."

These Christians, like all of us, came to Christ out of a "past." Now a past is a hard thing to shake. It is something you are always trying to "live up to" or "live down."

Some people are proud of their pasts, but most of us are prisoners to them. We are haunted by our pasts, hounded by them. We are haunted by the times we gave in, sold out or ran away. We are haunted by the thing we should have done but didn't, the place where we should have been but weren't, the habit we should have conquered but couldn't. You can run from the past, or you can live in the past, but you can never forget the past.

Perhaps we should not even try to forget it. The "baggage of by-gone days" can be a blessing as well as a burden. Since we cannot fully "leave it behind," perhaps, at least, we can learn from it. This is exactly what the writer of Hebrews was trying to get these Jewish Christians to do. Essentially, what he says is: "Remember the past, even regret the past, but whatever you do, do not repeat the past. You are your fathers' sons, but you do not need to practice your fathers' sins!" Breaking away from the past is not easy. It requires determination and courage. That's why so few people are able to do it.

It is said that those who do not know history are doomed to repeat it. Yet I have observed that those who do know history seem just as doomed to repeat it. “Their hearts are always going astray,” said God of their rebellious forefathers. He said it as if with shrugged shoulders and an incredulous sigh. Surely he must still be sighing. Stubbornly, we continue to “test” God’s justice and “try” his patience, with little or no appreciation of the lessons of the past. We barge into the future along the same dead-end streets of our predecessors. We go where they went, do what they did and pay the same price. You would think that we would learn.

One day, through the primeval wood
A calf walked home, as all calves should;
But made a trail all bent askew,
A crooked trail as all calves do.

Since then two hundred years have fled,
And, I infer, the calf is dead,
But still he left behind his trail,
And thereby hangs my moral tale.

The trail was taken up next day
By a lone dog that passed that way;
And then a wise bell-wether sheep
Pursued the trail o’er vale and steep….

And from that day, o’er hill and glade,
Through those old woods a path was made;
And many men wound in and out,
And dodged, and turned, and bent about
And uttered words of righteous wrath
Because ‘twas such a crooked path.

The forest path became a lane,
That bent, and turned, and turned again;
This crooked lane became a road,
Where many a poor horse with his load
Toiled on beneath the burning sun,
And traveled some three miles in one….

The years passed on in swiftness fleet,
The road became a village street;
And this, before men were aware,
A city's crowded thoroughfare;
And soon the central street was this
Of a renowned metropolis;

And o'er his crooked journey went
The traffic of a continent.
A hundred thousand men were led
By one calf near three centuries dead.
They followed still his crooked way,
And lost one hundred years a day;
For thus such reverence is lent
To well-established precedent....

For men are prone to go it blind
Along the calf paths of the mind,
And work away from sun to sun
To do what other men have done.[1]

Individual Christians, even entire congregations, can get lost on some winding path of yesterday. The path to renewal is not that kind of path. It is a straight path, a narrow one, and few there be who find it. Those who walk in it must be willing to break with precedent. They must be willing to see the past not as something to live in but as something to learn from.

If Christians are to be a renewable resource, not only must they learn from the past. They must also:

Long for the Promised

"There remains, then, a Sabbath-rest for the people of God" (Heb 4:9).

---

[1] From J. Wallace Hamilton, *Still the Trumpet Sounds* (Old Tappan, NJ: Revell), 172–73.

There is a sense in which Christianity is a religion of the "by-and-by." Though critics often scoff at this tense of our faith as "cowardly escapism," or so much "sentimental tripe," nothing is more basic to biblical Christianity than what it "hopes for the hereafter." The second coming, heaven, hell, punishment, reward are all major tenets of a faith that preaches, "This world is not my home." "Trust" and "hope" are future-tense verbs. Christians await, they expect, they anticipate what is to come.

The expectation which our author sets before the Hebrew Christians is one of the most inviting promises of the New Testament: rest. If there is anything these beleaguered Christians needed, it was rest. For them, Christianity had been work—hard work. Their faith had cost them dearly. Their discipleship had come at the price of public ridicule, confiscation of personal property, and for some, imprisonment. All of this had taken its toll. It had left them tired, the worst kind of tired—tired of struggling against a foe that will not go away, tired of wrestling with problems that seem to have no solution. It was the kind of fatigue that Julia Ward Howe once described as: "tired way down into the future."

This kind of fatigue can do strange things to us. It acts like a drug; it dulls the mind, weakens the will, diminishes our resolve. As Vince Lombardi once put it, "Fatigue makes cowards of us all." It can affect a whole generation, this kind of tiredness. It gets into the stuff of the mind, spreads like an epidemic, and becomes the prevailing mood of an age. It was true of that generation of their forefathers who got lost somewhere in the wilderness. Maybe it was the long years of slavery in Egypt, or perhaps it was the monotonous insecurity of the desert. But something had bleached the fight right out of them. They got tired quickly and were easily disheartened. They met problems with panic and obstacles with a murmur. Their dreams began to darken into doubts—doubts about Moses, about the promised land, and, most seriously, about the power of God. Fatigue deteriorated into faithlessness and "they fell along the way."

The writer sets this tragic model of unrealized rest before these tired Christians and urges them to "make every effort to enter that rest," which their forefathers never enjoyed.

The rest God promises is "rest from labor" (Heb 4:10). True rest always is. Rest instead of work is really no rest at all. It is escape, irresponsibility, unfaithfulness. Those who seek this kind of rest never find their way out of the wilderness. By contrast, rest from work suggests devotion and commitment. It is about accomplishment and fulfillment—the satisfaction of having expended effort towards the completion of some worthwhile task.

God's children still seek this kind of rest. There are some things we never quite finish this side of Canaan. We sew seeds of love in a hungry land and the weeds of hatred and indifference spring up to deny the harvest. We light lamps of brotherhood and understanding only to watch the cold winds of prejudice stir up to put them out. We strive to build our own Christian characters only to be frustrated at every turn. It is like trying to build a castle of sand on the shore of a pounding surf. Just about the time we put the finishing touches on our fortress of piety, a new wave of temptation washes it all away.

Like "fumbling apprentices," we also continue to work on our faith. We put in "overtime," trying to reconcile it to life. We struggle with the "unfair" tragedies which seem to contradict God's goodness. We wrestle with recurring feelings of guilt which seem to invalidate his forgiveness. We have our strength sapped by stubborn anxieties which seem to impede his peace. After awhile, we quietly begin to wonder if there will ever be an end to the chores of faith.

But the divine Foreman who supervises this great spiritual enterprise looks down on our efforts to offer a great promise: "You will rest from your labor." The unfinished tasks will be completed, the never-ending struggles will come to an end. We will leave them in the wilderness to enter our promised land. For the final time we will lay down the tools of our trade to rest with the satisfaction of knowing that the great work he has begun in us is finally completed.

There is an end to the career of faith—an end of finished work, fulfilled hope, and realized destiny. The future tense of Christianity is "future perfect" in every way.

Renewable Christians learn from the past and long for the promised. But they must also:

Live in the Present

"We have come to share in Christ if we hold firmly till the end the confidence we had at first" (Heb 3:14).

A wise pastor once responded to a bitter woman's resentful cry with words that capture the essence of Christianity as a "present-tense" religion. Angry at God over what had happened to her, she defiantly protested, "I wish I had never been made." The pastor replied, "You haven't been made, you are still being made!"

So it is in the Christian life. There is an existential dimension to our faith. There is a sense in which we are ever "becoming" Christian. In fact, the moment we begin to think that we "have become" Christian is the very moment we begin to "un-become" Christian. God is concerned about more than what we have done for him. He is concerned about what we have done for him lately. "Today," insists our author, "Today, if you will hear his voice, do not harden your heart." It is as if God keeps his finger on our "spiritual pulse," continually monitoring our "vital signs." Refusing to let us "rest on our laurels," he continually confronts us with some moment of truth to which we must respond. He expects us to keep the faith.

According to the author of Hebrews the responses God seeks from us are two, the combination of which the author calls "faithfulness." They are *faith*—believing God's promises, taking him at his word—and *obedience*—answering his call, giving heed to his commands. Some theologians insist these responses are in *tension*. Here, they are in *tandem*. For the author of Hebrews, "faithfulness" is "behavior consistent with belief." It is remaining true to one's convictions, or as he says it in 3:14, "holding firmly to our confidence."

"Believe" and "obey" are present-tense verbs. They are what we do between Egypt and Canaan—in the wilderness that lies between redemption and final rest. For somewhere along the way God will come calling. After the desert has taken its toll and the manna no longer satisfies, when our drive has deserted us and our dreams have begun to fade, he will come calling. He will expect us to finish what we have started, to renew our commitment, to go on to Canaan, on to reward, on to rest.

An old missionary couple had been working in Africa for years and were returning to New York City to retire. They had no pension; their health was broken; they were defeated, discouraged, and afraid. They discovered they were booked on the same ship as President Teddy Roosevelt, who was returning from one of his big-game hunting expeditions.

No one paid any attention to them. They watched the fanfare that accompanied the President's entourage, with passengers trying to catch a glimpse of the great man.

As the ship moved across the ocean, the old missionary said to his wife, "Something is wrong. Why should we have given our lives in faithful service for God in Africa these many years and have no one care a thing about us? Here this man comes back from a hunting trip and everybody makes much over him. But nobody gives two hoots about us."

"Dear, you shouldn't feel that way," his wife said.

"I can't help it; it doesn't seem right."

When the ship docked in New York, a band was waiting to greet the President. The mayor and other dignitaries were there. The papers were full of the President's arrival, but no one noticed this missionary couple. They slipped off the ship and found a cheap flat on the East Side, hoping the next day to see what they could do to make a living in the city.

That night the man's spirit broke. He said to his wife, "I can't take this; God is not treating us fairly."

His wife replied, "Why don't you go into the bedroom and tell that to the Lord?"

A short time later he came out from the bedroom, but now his face was completely different. His wife asked, "Dear, what happened?"

"The Lord settled it with me," he said. "I told him how bitter I was that the President should receive this tremendous homecoming, while no one met us as we returned home. And when I finished, it seemed as though the Lord put his hand on my shoulder and simply said, 'But you're not home yet!'"[2]

And neither are we.

[2] Ray Stedman, *Talking to My Father,* condensed in "To Illustrate…," *Leadership* 8.3 (Summer 1987) 48.

CHAPTER 11

Early Christian Apocalyptic: A Comparison Between the New Testament Book of Revelation and the Apocryphal Apocalypse of Peter

DAVID A. FIENSY

We can often understand texts better by comparing and contrasting them with other texts of similar content or genre. For instance, it is instructive to compare the laws of the Pentateuch with the Code of Hammurabi. Fruitful results can follow a study of Paul's letters in light of the form and structure of other ancient letters. It is also helpful to place the book of Acts beside other contemporaneous Hellenistic histories. Comparisons demonstrate the commonality of the texts in method. For example, Paul's letters usually follow the same general outline as other ancient letters. When one of his letters does not—the epistle to the Galatians, for instance, has no thanksgiving expressed for the recipients, a common element in most ancient letters—we can be fairly certain that he has had a good reason for deviating from the normal practice. On the other hand, comparisons also point out differences: Paul greets his readers with the phrase, "grace and peace," instead of the usual Greek greeting.

The book of Revelation (= R) also becomes clearer when compared with other literature of a similar type. R is an apocalypse and as such should be compared with Jewish apocalypses such as 4 Ezra, 2 Baruch, 2 Enoch, and the Apocalypse of Abraham. These apocalypses contain accounts of visions, symbolic numbers, symbolic animal figures, huge beasts, and the coming end of the age like R. But R is a Christian apocalypse which stresses the "lamb that was slain" and that stress makes it a remarkably singular apocalypse. Unlike the Jewish apocalypses, the Messiah has already come for John, the author of R. For John, that Messiah has been slain, and the saints have washed their garments in his blood. Yet the same slain lamb will return as victorious conqueror.

The subject of this essay, however, is the comparison between two Christian apocalypses: R and the nearly contemporaneous so-called Apocalypse of Peter.[1] We say "so-called" because the Apocalypse of Peter (= AP) is certainly pseudonymous. The date of this apocalypse (see below) makes it impossible for the apostle Peter to have written it. Yet it is one of the earliest Christian apocalypses and thus provides us with a mirror of at least some Christian communities in the mid-second century A.D.. Although the two books were written nearly contemporaneously, R was accepted into the canon and AP was not. What is there about the history and content of the two works that may explain this difference and in the process help us define R more clearly?

1. Definition of Apocalyptic

Apocalyptic literature is somewhat easier to recognize than to define. Nevertheless, the best definition is probably that of J. J. Collins which can be paraphrased as follows: An apocalypse is a written document which describes how a revelation was made from God to a human being through an angel. The revelation can be about the future (temporal revelation) or about the heavens as they are now (spatial revelation).[2] D.S. Russell, in his now classic description of apocalyptic literature, lists three important characteristics of apocalyptic literature:[3]

1. Apocalypses are "esoteric in character." That is, they claim to be disclosing secrets. The secrets often were, it is alleged, written on heavenly tablets (e.g. 1 Enoch 81:2; Testament of Asher 7:5).

---

[1] One must distinguish this text from the Coptic Apocalypse of Peter found at Nag Hammadi in Egypt. These two Apocalypses of Peter have no relationship to each other. The Shepherd of Hermas, dating from around A.D. 140 would also make an interesting comparative study but that must await a future paper.

[2] J. J. Collins, "Introduction: Towards the Morphology of a Genre," in *idem*, ed., *Apocalypse, the Morphology of a Genre*; *Semeia* 14 (1979) 1–9.

[3] D.S. Russell, *The Method and Message of Jewish Apocalyptic* (Philadelphia: Westminster, 1964) 104–39. Russell actually lists five characteristics but the three given above are most important.

2. These literary products are highly symbolic in language. Many of the symbols are taken from the Old Testament and others from ancient Near Eastern mythology. There are sea monsters (Testament of Asher 7:3; 1 Enoch 60:7–9; 4 Ezra 6:49–52), great beasts (4 Ezra 13:2), bulls (1 Enoch 85–86), sheep (1 Enoch 89:16), and many other animals. There are stars and other cosmic luminaries (1 Enoch 87:2; Testament of Levi 8:2) and numbers (especially the numbers 3, 4, 7, 10, and 12 and multiples of these numbers).

3. Apocalypses are literary in form. They are written documents. While the prophetic movements in the first century were oral, the apocalyptic movement was literary. Writing down revelation, the secrets, is usually commanded of the recipient (Testament of Moses 1:16).

Collins divides the apocalypses into two categories: apocalypses with historical reviews and apocalypses with heavenly journeys—of course some apocalypses contain both.[4] The first type contains in highly symbolic language a review of the major events from the exile to the author's own time (2 Baruch). The second type describes a journey through the various levels of heaven (2 Enoch), a journey through the various parts of the cosmos where weather is made and the stars and other heavenly bodies originate (1 Enoch), or a journey through the place the spirits of the dead are inhabiting (1 Enoch).

Our two main texts of interest, R and AP—though there are elements of both kinds of apocalyptic in each text—fit into the historical review and heavenly journey respectively. R has a historical review in chapter 13 and 17 in the symbol of the beast with the seven heads and ten horns which represent the Roman emperors. In addition, R has a repetitive cycle of judgment expressed in the three sevens: the seven seals, trumpets, and bowls. These describe the judgment which has happened and is about to happen to the cosmos. AP on the other hand is in the main a vision of Hell and Heaven. Peter is allowed to see the punishments of the wicked and then the reward of the righteous. Thus our two apocalypses are of essentially different types.

---

[4] Collins, *Apocalypse*, 10–19.

2. Summary of the Apocalypse of Peter

Since the text of AP is not readily available and not commonly known, it may be helpful at the outset to give a summary of its contents. In addition, a lengthy passage is quoted in section 6 of this essay:

> While sitting on the mount of Olives, Jesus is asked about the signs of his coming and the end of the world. Jesus replies that there will be false Christs (Matt 24:5). Jesus will come on the clouds as lightning with a heavenly host. His cross will go before him. He will shine seven times brighter than the sun. He will come with all his saints and angels. Then he will receive a crown from the father and will judge the living and the dead.
>
> When Jesus repeats the parable of the fig tree (Mark 13:28), Peter asks what it means. Jesus answers that the fig tree is Israel. When the boughs sprout, false Christs shall come. Many will turn away after them and deny the one they crucified. If they reject the false Christ, he will kill them with a dagger. Then Enoch and Elijah will come to warn that this is not the Messiah.
>
> Jesus then shows Peter in Jesus' own right palm a vision of what the last day will be like. The righteous and sinners will be separated. The sinners will weep in sorrow so much that everyone else will behold them and weep, the righteous, angels, even Jesus himself. Peter says it would have been better if sinners had not been born (cf. 4 Ezra). Jesus rebukes Peter for this saying. Jesus says no one has more compassion for "his image" than God, for he created them out of nothing. Next Jesus shows the evil works which the sinners did to warrant such punishment.
>
> But next the text speaks about what "they" will experience in the last days when the "day of God" comes. At the day of judgment will be a resurrection by the fiat of God (similar to Ezekiel 37). Uriel will give the soul and spirit to the flesh (1 Enoch 20:1).
>
> These are the punishments in that day for those who have fallen away from faith and sinned: cataracts of fire, darkness, water becomes fire.
>
> Christ will come on a cloud with the angels. The father will put a crown on his head. When the nations see it, they will weep, each

nation for itself. He will command them to go into the river of fire but not the elect. Next comes a description of the various punishments (see below section VI) which forms the major part of the book (chapters 6–14 out of a total of 17).

Then a scene resembling the transfiguration of Christ in the gospels takes place. Moses and Elijah appear in celestial form, extremely radiant. When Peter asks about Abraham, Isaac, and Jacob, he sees a vision of paradise, full of beautiful trees, fruits, and perfumes. After the voice from heaven says, "This is my son," a cloud bears away Jesus, Moses and Elijah to the second heaven.

3. The Manuscripts of Each Text

Fragments of the AP in Greek are extant in patristic quotations (Clement of Alexandria and Theophilus of Antioch); the Bodleian leaf, acquired in 1894; the Akhmim fragment, discovered in a tomb in Akhmim, Egypt in 1887; and the Rainer fragment, acquired in 1880 but only brought to light in 1924. The full text of the AP is only extant in one Ethiopic ms discovered in 1907.[5] The Bodleian and Rainer fragments are dated to the third to the fifth centuries A.D.. The Akhmim fragment is no earlier than the eighth century A.D..[6]

One of the first questions scholars asked about the AP was the relation of the Akhmim text, the largest of the fragments, to the original AP.

---

[5] For the Greek texts of everything except the Bodleian and Rainer fragments see E. Klostermann, *Apocrypha I* (Berlin: Walter de Gruyter, 1933). The Greek of the Bodlein is in M. R. James, "A New Text of the Apocalypse of Peter II" *Journal of Theological Studies* 12 (1910–11) 367–68. For the Greek of the Rainer fragment see K. Pruemm, "De genuino apocalypsis Petri textu," *Biblica* 10 (1929) 78. For the Ethiopic text see M. S. Gre'baut, *Revue de l'Orient Chretien*, 1910. Translations of all except the Rainer fragment can be found in M. R. James, *The Apocryphal New Testament* (Oxford: Clarendon, 1945) 505–21. All of the fragments and texts are translated in E. Hennecke, W. Schneemelcher, and R. McL. Wilson, *New Testament Apocrypha* (Philadelphia: Westminster, 1964) 2.663–683. There is also an Arabic text.

[6] For the dates of the Bodleian and Rainer fragments see M. R. James, "The Rainer Fragment of the Apocalypse of Peter" *Journal of Theological Studies* 32 (1931) 278. For the date of the Akhmim text see J. R. Harris, *Gospel of Peter* (New York: James Pott, 1893) 16. The Akhmim tomb also contained in the same binding the Gospel of Peter and Greek 1 Enoch.

A. Dieterich and T. Zahn were convinced even before the Ethiopic text was found that the Akhmim fragment was not just a piece of the AP but a section of the Gospel of Peter with which it was found.[7] They argued that most of the patristic quotations were too dissimilar to the Akhmim to be quotations of it.

The discovery of the Ethiopic text helped to confirm the conclusion that the Akhmim was not a copy of the AP. The Akhmim and Ethiopic, where roughly parallel in story, are often very different in details. On the other hand the patristic quotations of the AP and the other fragments are most like the Ethiopic. A significant similarity among the Ethiopic fragments is the casting of the visions in the form of a prophecy. In the Akhmim Peter sees what is happening at present in Hell and Paradise while in the Ethiopic text Peter sees a vision of what will happen in those places. Thus we have two recensions of AP: The Ethiopic and all of the early fragments and quotations from the church fathers comprise one and the Akhmim comprises the other. M. R. James concluded, therefore, that the Ethiopic was closer to the AP known to the early church than the Akhmim. We can accept James' conclusion since few have challenged it.[8] Therefore, we will not use the Akhmim text in our comparison.

The text of R is based on 301 Greek mss of which only three are complete (i.e. containing all of R). The oldest and most important of these are as follows:[9]

1. P^{18} containing 1:4–7 and dating to the late third to early fourth century.

2. P^{24} containing 5:5–8 and 6:5–8 and dates to the early fourth century.

3. P^{47} containing 9:10–17:2 and dating to the late third century.

---

[7] Dieterich, *Nekyia* (Stuttgart: Teuber, 1969 [1893]) 14; Zahn, *Grundriss des Geschichte des neutestamentliche Kanons*, cited by M. R. James, "A New Text III," *Journal of Theological Studies* 12 (1910–11) 578.

[8] See James, "A New Text III," 573–83; and idem. "The Rainer Fragment," 270–79. L. Vaganay (*L'Evangile de Pierre* [Paris: Gabalda, 1930] 187–92) is one of the few who has challenged James' conclusion.

[9] The following information is based on D. Aune, *Revelation 1–5* (Word Biblical Commentary; Dallas: Word Books, 1997) cxxvi-cxlviii.

4. P^{98} containing 1:13–20 and dating to the second century (thus making it the oldest witness to the text of R). The first four mss listed are papyrus texts.

5. Codex Sinaiticus (א) which dates to the fourth century. This uncial text (written in all capital letters) written on leather is the oldest complete text of R.

6. Codex Alexandrinus (A) which dates from the fifth century. This (also an uncial written on parchment) is the second oldest complete text of R.

We may summarize the comparison between the manuscript testimony of these two texts as follows:

	Greek mss	**Complete mss**	**Earliest ms**
Apoc. of Peter	3	0	third century
Revelation	301	3	second century

It is also interesting to note that AP is much shorter than R. According to the stichometry (numbers of lines) given in the sixth century Claromontanus manuscript (known as D), R had 1200 lines and AP only 270 lines. Thus R is more than four times the length of the original AP.

4. The Date, Provenance and Sitz im Leben *of the Two Texts*

The date of AP is generally agreed upon. Patristic quotations from the end of the second century provide a *terminus ad quem* (time up to which or latest possible date). The earliest quotations are those of Theophilus of Antioch (A.D. 180) and Clement of Alexandria (A.D. 215). James also believed he could find allusions to AP in the Shepherd of Hermas (A.D. 140) though these references are not as clearly present.[10] The *terminus post quem* (time after which or earliest possible date) is A.D. 100 since AP alludes to several passages in 4 Ezra which was composed at the end of the first century.[11] In addition, the first two chapters

[10] See James, "New Text II," 381–83.

[11] The allusions are in AP chapter 3 according to Hennecke's chapter divisions (*New Testament Apocrypha*, 2.670). The passages of 4 Ezra are 4:12, 5:33, and 7:46.

of AP (cited according to Hennecke's divisions) refer to a false Christ, a deceiver. He will martyr those who refuse to follow him. If this refers to Bar Kosiba (Bar Cochba) it would date the document to about A.D. 135.[12]

The provenance (or place of writing) of AP is considerably more difficult to discover. C. Mauer and A. Yarbrough-Collins argued that the reference to reverence for animals in chapter 10 of AP together with the testimony to the AP by Clement of Alexandria (in Egypt) points to an Egyptian provenance.[13] In Egypt people were especially known for their worship of animals. But other geographical areas are represented among the quotations (e.g. Antioch of Syria) and the reverence for animals need not be limited to Egypt.[14] The allusion to Bar Kosiba would seem to point to Palestine or at least Syria as the provenance. The author speaks as if the persecution of Bar Kosiba were a real part of his or his community's experience.

It is generally accepted that R was written toward the close of Domitian's reign (around A.D. 96) and in the area of Asia Minor.[15] Irenaeus

---

[12] So argues C. Mauer in Hennecke, *New Testament Apocrypha*, 2.664; M. Erbetta, *Gli Apocrifi del Nuovo Testamento* (Marietti, 1969) 3.214; W. Michaelis, *Die Apokryphen Schriften zum Neuen Testament* (Bremen: Schunemann, 1956) 474; and A. Yarbro Collins, "Early Christian Apocalypses," in J.J. Collins, ed., *Apocalypse: The Morphology of a Genre*, 72. J. R. Harris ("The Odes of Solomon and the Apocalypse of Peter" *Expository Times* 42 [1930] 21–23) has attempted to demonstrate that AP antedates R, 1 and 2 John and the Odes of Solomon, all of which (alleges Harris) have used a verse from AP. But Harris inexplicably used the Arabic text of AP, failed to recognize the quotation of 4 Ezra in the Ethiopic version, and ignored the argument of F. Spitta, "Die Petrusapokalypse und der zweite Petrusbrief" *Zeitschrift für die Neuentestamentliche Wissenschaft* 12 (1911) 237–42, which was that AP has used 2 Peter. A. Bardenhewer has expanded Spitta's argument (*Geschichte der altkirchlichen Literatur* [Freiberg: Briesgau, 1912–24] 613).

[13] Mauer in Hennecke, *New Testament Apocrypha*, 2.664; Yarbro Collins, "Early Christian Apocalypses," 72.

[14] G. Quispel and R. M. Grant argue that Clement of Alexandria was introduced to AP in Palestine ("Note on the Petrine Apocrypha" *Vigiliae Christianae* 6 [1952] 31–32).

[15] "Practically all of the early Christian writers place (Revelation) toward the very end of the reign of Domitian, who died in A.D. 96, a date that is accepted by most modern students of the question," M. Rist, "Revelation" *Interpreter's Bible* (New York: Abingdon, 1957) 12.354. See also R.H. Charles, *Revelation of St. John* (Edinburgh: T. & T.

in A.D. 180 wrote that John wrote the Revelation "at the close of Domitian's reign" (*Haer.* 5.30.3). In addition the emperor worship which was zealously practiced first during the reign of Domitian fits the references of persecution within the text of R (13:4–10, 13–15). The provenance seems settled because of the reference to Patmos (R 1:9), an island just off the coast of Asia Minor, and because of the letters to the seven Asian churches (R 2–3). The Neronian persecution cannot probably explain the situation of R since Nero's persecution did not extend to Asia but remained localized to the vicinity of Rome.[16]

Thus the two apocalypses are separated by about forty years and come from different geographical settings. R is the earlier of the two apocalypses.

	Date	**Provenance**
Apoc. of Peter	A.D. 135	Syria or Egypt
Revelation	A.D. 96	Asia Minor

The *Sitz im Leben* or situation in life of the AP was apparently one of persecution. In chapters 1 and 2 of AP a false Christ and deceiver is described and the saints who deny the false Christ and cling to the "first Christ whom they crucified" are martyred. Chapters 9 and 16 also refer to persecution. These references suggest that Christians who have refused to follow Bar Kosiba have been attacked by him. Bar Kosiba claimed to be the Messiah and persecuted Christians that would not reject Jesus and accept him.[17] Yet the persecution does not appear to be as

Clark, 1920) 1.xliii, xcv; R. Brown, *New Testament Introduction* (New York: Doubleday, 1997) 805–09; D. Aune, *Revelation 1–5*, lvi-lxx. Aune maintains that the book was published in two editions: the first in the sixties A.D. and the second at the time of Domitian.

[16] The attempt of J. M. Ford to date R before A.D. 70 has found little support (see Aune above) among early Christian writers since none alleged a pre-70 date. Ford placed R in the context of Nero's persecution. See J. M. Ford, *Revelation* (Garden City: Doubleday, 1975) 51–56.

[17] Justin Martyr, *Apology* 1.31, tells about the persecution of Christians. For accounts of Bar Kosiba's rebellion see Dio Cassius, *Roman History* 69.12–14; and Eusebius, *Ecclesiastical History* 4.6; j. Taanit 4.6; b. Gittin 57a. See also the letters of Bar Kosiba published by J. A. Fitzmyer and D. J. Harrington, *A Manual of Palestinian Aramaic Texts* (Rome: Biblical Institute Press, 1978). For secondary works on Bar Kosiba

severe in the community of AP as in the churches associated with R. In R the slain cry out for justice (6:9) while one of the main functions of paradise in R is to comfort the martyrs (7:11–17; 21:4). Domitian's persecution was probably more systematic and severe. There seems to have been more martyrs in the churches of Asia Minor during the writing of R.

5. Use of the Two Apocalypses in the Early Church

The AP was held in high esteem by some in the second and third centuries. Clement of Alexandria regarded it as a canonical writing (Eusebius, *E.H.* 6.14.1). It is listed in the Muratorian Canon but with the explanation, "Some will not have it read in church." Sozomen (7.19) who lived in the fifth century observed that some churches in Palestine still read the AP on Good Friday. It seems to have been read especially in Egypt where it was translated from Greek into both Ethiopic and Arabic.[18] On the other hand, Eusebius (fourth century) declared that the "catholic tradition" did not accept the AP for orthodox writers have not used its testimonies (*E.H.* 3.3.2). Jerome (fifth century) affirmed that it should not be accepted as canonical (*de vir. Ill.* 1).

R was also widely read but had at least three detractors. The earliest allusion to R is in Justin Martyr. He quoted R and attributed its authorship to John the Apostle. Irenaeus (A.D. 180) quoted R at least five times and again mentions John the Apostle as the author. Both Clement of Alexandria and Theophilus of Antioch referred to and cited R as inspired scripture. The Muratorian Canon also indicates that by the end of the second century A.D., R was accepted by the church generally as part of the New Testament canon. Thus R was clearly known and widely read and quoted as canonical in the early church.[19]

---

see: E. M. Smallwood, *The Jews Under Roman Rule* (Leiden: Brill, 1976) 440; H. Mantel, "The Causes of the Bar Kokba Revolt" *Jewish Quarterly Review* 58 (1967) 224–42, 274–96; E. Schürer, *A History of the Jewish People* (New York: Schocken, 1967) 293–308.

[18] J. Quasten, *Patrology* (Westminster, Maryland: Christian Classics, 1992) 1.144. Ch. Mauer, in Hennecke, *New Testament Apocrypha*, 2.664.

[19] M. Tenney, *Interpreting Revelation* (Grand Rapids, Michigan: Eerdmans, 1957) 16–17.

Nevertheless, Gaius, a presbyter of Rome in A.D. 200 disliked the millennial teachings of R and surmised that all of the Johannine literature was written by one Cerinthus, the archheretic (Eusebius, *E.H.* 3.28.2). Gaius and his followers were called "the alogoi" because they rejected the *logos* doctrine of Johannine literature. In addition, Dionysius of Alexandria who was deeply influenced by Greek philosophy and also opposed to millennialism or chiliasm, also challenged the apostolic authorship of revelation (Eusebius, *E.H.* 7.25). Dionysius argued that the vocabulary and style of Revelation were different from the Gospel and epistles. Thus Dionysius concluded that another person named John wrote Revelation while John the apostle wrote the Gospel and epistles. Finally, Eusebius also had doubts about R but this may have been based on his dislike of millennialism. Yet as Eusebius makes clear, the church in general had accepted R as canonical by the early fourth century. As M. Tenney noted, by the fourth century A.D., R appears in most of the canon lists officially given by the councils of the church. On the other hand no other apocalypses—including the AP—were included in such lists (the one listing of AP in the table below is not from an official council list).[20]

One should conclude from all of this that although AP was read in the early church, especially in Egypt, by the fourth century it was largely abandoned. As B. Metzger terms it, AP had local and temporary canonicity while R had universal canonicity.[21] On the other hand, although R was doubted by a few people by the fourth century it was largely accepted as canonical and inspired. We can summarize the early canon lists with reference to R and AP as follows:

[20] Ibid.

[21] B.M. Metzger, *The Canon of the New Testament* (Oxford: Clarendon Press, 1987) 165.

Early Canon Lists[22]

	Irenaeus	Tertullian	Clement	Muratorian	Origen
Apoc. Pet.	0	0	X	?	0
Rev	X	X	X	X	X

Later Canon Lists[23]

	1	2	3	4	5	6	7	8	9
Apoc. Pet	X	0	0	0	0	0	0	0	*
R	X	0	X	X	0	0	?	X	X

Key: X = included; 0 = not mentioned; ? = disputed;
* = considered spurious

Thus only one of the later canon lists (and that is not from an official council) names AP but most of them name R. Due probably to the distaste at that time for millenarianism, some were hesitant with regard to R yet the majority of the churches considered R inspired scripture. Even in an intellectual climate of difficulty for a book like R, it had the support of the majority of the churches. This observation should indicate the strength of the tradition about the inspiration of R. On the other hand, the decreasing use of AP is striking.

6. Theological Emphasis of Each Apocalypse

We give only the more striking comparisons here. First, both apocalypses are *similar* in that they are concerned with the parousia

[22] See D. A. Fiensy, *New Testament Introduction* (Joplin, MO: College Press, 1994) 370. The dates for the sources are as follows: Irenaeus (A.D. 180); Tertullian (A.D. 200); Clement of Alexandria (A.D. 200); Muratorian Canon (A.D. 190); Origen (A.D. 220).

[23] See Metzger, *Canon*, 310–315. In the table number 1 = Canon in Codex Claromontanus (fifth century A.D.); 2 = Canon of Cyril of Jerusalem (A.D. 350); 3 = Cheltenham Canon (A.D. 360); 4 = Canon of Athanasius (A.D. 367); 5 = Canon of the Apostolic Constitutions (A.D. 380); 6 = Canon of Gregory of Nazianzus (A.D. 350); 7 = Canon of Amphilochius of Iconium (A.D. 400); 8 = Canon of the Council of Carthage (A.D. 397); 9 = Eusebius (A.D. 325).

(second coming of Christ). AP begins with a question about signs of the parousia (modeled after Matthew 24) in chapter 1. In chapter 2 the signs are explained. When Israel becomes unfruitful, and when a false Christ produces martyrs, the parousia is near. The intention is obvious: the reader is supposed to conclude that those signs are now present; thus the end is imminent. Yet the author loses interest in the second coming of Christ when he turns to the judgment (chapter 6). This leads to a detailed description of the various punishments. The scene next changes in chapter 15 to the transfiguration story of the synoptics (Mark 9 and parallels). This quickly shifts to a vision of paradise (chapter 16) where the blessed abide. After this vision, Jesus, Moses, and Elijah, all who had appeared on the mount of transfiguration, ascend into heaven (chapter 17). Nothing more is said of the parousia after chapter 6.

In R the emphasis on the parousia remains throughout and closes with strong affirmation of its importance and imminence (R 20:6–7, 12, 20).

Second, the scenarios are roughly the same in each apocalypse if we omit from consideration for the moment the great differences in judgment and punishment in them. We begin in each (AP chapters 1–2; R 1–3) with the emphasis on the imminence of the parousia and its significance for the present situation. Next we are introduced to a series of woes or punishments (R 6–16; AP 6–14). We end with paradise (R 21–22; AP 16–17).

Third, both AP and R wish to emphasize that God is just in his judgment and punishment of sins. The AP alludes to Psalm 19:9 twice (chapters 7 and 13) as does R (16:7; 19:2) to explain God's severe chastisement of sinners. AP shows concern over the punishments of the wicked. As was noted above, 4 Ezra 4:12, 5:33, and 7:46 are alluded to in chapter 3 of AP. Peter questions the fairness of such harsh punishments much the way Ezra did and receives a similar reply. Furthermore, an escape from punishment is provided if the elect intercede on behalf of the wicked (chapter 14). This reduces hell to a quasi-purgatory. The idea of eternal punishment is also in AP (chapters 5–7, 11) as well as the notion that after the judgment one can no longer find forgiveness (chapter 13). The notions are thus in tension with one another. This tension may be due to the source or sources of AP. A Jewish source is probably represented by the notion of the finality of judgment, while the author of AP may have inserted his belief in the purging function of hell. The idea of purgatory appears to have come originally from the pagan Orphic religion. It emerges in Judaism in the second century A.D. about the same time as or a little later than AP.[24] The concept in AP, however, is not exactly the same as in Judaism. In AP the wicked are released from punishment if the elect request it. In Judaism—as in Orphism—the wicked are released after they have been punished sufficiently.

R, although also expressing concern for the punishment of the wicked, on the other hand knows of no escape from hell (14:11). Those who are punished after death are punished eternally; judgment is final.

One of the great *differences* between the two apocalypses is that AP has great interest in telling what the punishments of the wicked will be after the judgment. We quote here a sampling:

> 7. Then will men and women come to the place prepared for them. By their tongues with which they have blasphemed the way of righteousness will they be hung up. There is spread out for them unquenchable fire.... And again two women: they are hung up by their neck and by their hair and are cast into the pit. These are they who plaited their hair, not to create beauty, but to turn to fornication, and that they might ensnare the souls of men to destruction. And the men who lay with them in fornication are hung by their thighs in that burning place, and they say to one another, "We did not know that we would come into everlasting torture."... 8. And near this flame there is a great and very deep pit and into it there flow all kinds of things from everywhere: judgment (?), horrifying things and excretions. And the women are swallowed up by this up to their necks and are punished with great pain. These are they who have

[24] For Orphism, see Plato, *Phaedo* 111 D-E; Pindar, *Odes* 2.56–130 and Dieterich, *Nekyia*. One of the problems in studying Orphism is that, because no Orphic books are extant, one depends on excerpts of Orphic teachings in Plato, Pindar, Empedocles, Virgil, the tragedians, Christians writers and others. For a collection of such excerpts, see O. Kern, *Orphicorum Fragmenta* (Berlin: Weidmanns, 1922). For purgatory in Judaism see H. Strack and P. Billerbeck, *Kommentar zum neuen Testament aus Talmud und Midrasch* (München: Beck, 1928) 4.1043–49. Strack and Billerbeck cite many references to a purgatory teaching in the rabbinic literature, e.g., b. Rosh haShana 16b.

> procured abortions and have ruined the work of God which he has created. Opposite them is another place where the children sit, but both alive, and they cry to God. And lightnings go forth from those children which pierce the eyes of those who, by fornication, have brought about their destruction....[25]

Some have argued that influences from the Orphic religion—which taught reincarnation and intermediate punishments/purgings—on the mind of the author of AP have produced this description of hell (or purgatory?).[26] Others maintain that a Jewish source, although perhaps at some distant point in the past influenced by Orphism, stands behind this part of AP.[27] At any rate, the gruesome interest in the punishments of the wicked (AP chapters 6–14) finds no place in R. In R punishment in the lake of fire (20:15) is only briefly mentioned. The details of punishment might on the other hand be roughly paralleled with the woes which will come on earth prior to the parousia in R (see R chapters 6–16). But these judgments are on the cosmos in general and describe no individual's torment.

Second, the literary setting is also different in each apocalypse. The occasion for the scenes of hell and paradise in AP are two Synoptic pericopae: one the eschatological discourse in Matthew 24 and the other the transfiguration scene in Mark 9 and parallels. R on the other hand begins as an epistle—or more precisely seven epistles—but becomes a vision of the future. Second, John is enraptured to heaven (R 4:1) to receive his revelation. In AP the first vision occurs when Jesus shows the disciples in the palm of his hand the judgment and subsequent punishments

---

[25] Translation from H. Duensing in Hennecke, *New Testament Apocrypha*, II, 672–673.

[26] See A. Dieterich, *Nekyia*; W. K. C. Guthrie, *Orpheus and Greek Religion* (London: Methuen, 1952) 216–20; W. Michaelis, *Die Apokyrphen Schriften zum Neuen Testament* (Bremen: Schunemann, 1956) 475.

[27] See D. A. Fiensy, "*Lex Talionis* in the Apocalypse of Peter" *Harvard Theological Review* 74 (1981) 255–58; A. Marmarstein, "Jüdische Parallelen zur Petrusapokalypse" *Zeitschrift für die Neuentestamentliche Wissenschaft* 10 (1909) 297–300; M. Gaster, "Hebrew Visions of Hell and Paradise," *Studies and Texts* (London: Maggs, 1925–28) 1.124–64.

(chapter 3). The second vision in AP occurs when upon the mount of transfiguration Peter asks to see where the patriarchs are. Next follows: "And he showed us a garden" (chapter 16). It is not clear how or where this vision was seen.

Third, a striking difference is the absence of millennialism in AP. R (20:1–7) is parallel to what Jewish apocalyptists were teaching at the end of the first century (2 Baruch 40:3; 2 Enoch 32:2–33:2; 4 Ezra 7:28–29). AP cannot have been ignorant of this tradition since he certainly alludes to 4 Ezra (see above). Why does AP ignore the millennium as a concept? He seems more interested in what happens after the judgment than before. He also ignores the woes listed in Matthew (which he used in the first chapter) which were supposed to precede the parousia. None of these calamities are as important for AP as the final judgment and subsequent punishments. There is a very short version of cosmic woes in AP chapter 5, something roughly like those of R 6–16, but these are quickly passed over in favor of the post-judgment punishments. The only event prior to judgment which AP is really interested in is the appearance of a false Christ, the very situation in which he was living. AP's extreme interest in the punishments and to some extent rewards after death was probably a disciplinary method. In other words, the author wanted to control and discipline his community by frightening them with punishments in the afterlife. In addition, AP may represent an early distaste for millennialism literally interpreted, a feeling that would eventually predominate in the Western church but also was supported by some in the Eastern church.[28]

Fourth, the most significant difference between R and AP is the strong Christocentric emphasis in R. The tone for R is set in 1:8 when the exalted Christ says, "I am the alpha and omega…the one who is, was, and is coming, the omnipotent." This saying is echoed at the end of the book (22:13), "I am the alpha and omega, the first and last, beginning and end." Christ, the omnipotent (Greek: παντοκράτωρ [*pantokratôr*]),

[28] In the west Augustine's spiritualizing of the millennium in the *City of God* became standard. Origen and Dionysius of Alexandria were two eastern opponents of millennialism.

stands as exalted Lord over the cosmos. All that happens in between these two statements ultimately focuses on him and his eternal reign.

R consists in the main of four visions.[29] Each of these visions has a theme which concerns the Lordship of Christ:

Vision I: Christ the Lord of the Church (1:9–3:22)
Vision II: Christ the Lord of History (4:1–16:21)
Vision III: Christ the Lord of Judgment (17:1–21:8)
Vision IV: Christ the Lord of the New Jerusalem (21:9–22:5)

As M. Tenney has observed, Christ appears in the first vision as the Deity who oversees the church. He is the observer of the churches who moves constantly among them to preserve his saints and rebuke the sinners. He is the one who infallibly discerns the hearts of those in the churches. He is the final authority who can remove a lampstand. And he is the one whose personal return the churches long for and pray for.[30]

In vision two Christ controls history and brings it to its conclusion. A little book is presented before the throne of God. A mighty angel asks who is worthy to open the scroll and break the seven seals. The Lamb that was slain comes forward and is acclaimed worthy to receive the scroll and break the seals. The heavenly choir sings of his worthiness; he is worthy because he has been slain (5:6–10). As he breaks each new seal, things begin to take place both on earth and in the heavens. Wars, famines, death, and other events take place. When the seventh seal is opened, it brings the seven trumpets which produce yet more events such as those of the seals. The Dragon and the two Beasts attempt to foil the Lamb's design but are ineffective. Finally, angels appear again and sing the song of the Lamb. After this song they begin to pour out their seven bowls, each bringing wrath like the seals and trumpets before them. This continual refrain about the Lamb that was slain marks a decisive difference between R and Jewish apocalypses. The latter have a notion of a conquering Messiah who destroys enemies of Israel or the wicked within Israel with the sword of his mouth or the like (see 4 Ezra, 2 Baruch, 1 Enoch [Similitudes], Sibylline Oracles). But in R the Messiah conquers

---

[29] This section is developed from Tenney, *Interpreting Revelation*, 117–34.

[30] Tenney, *Interpreting Revelation*, 124–25.

precisely because he has been slain; he conquers by means of his death. The Christian kerygma has so affected John that his apocalypse can never be considered in the same way as Jewish apocalypses.

After the Dragon and two Beasts make war against the Lamb, they are judged and cast down (17–18). No one can resist the might of the Lamb. He enters victoriously on his white horse, the judge of the cosmos. As a judge he is Faithful and True (19:11); he is the Word of God (19:13); he is the King of Kings and Lord of Lords (19:16).

Last comes the vision of the new Jerusalem. Here the Lamb is the bridegroom of the people of God who are represented as his wife (21:9); the foundations of the city are inscribed with the names of the apostles of the Lamb (21:14); worship in a temple is unnecessary since the Lord God Omnipotent and the Lamb have become the new temple (21:22); no light is necessary since the Lamb is the light of the new Jerusalem (21:23); the saints are insured of salvation by having their names enrolled in the Lamb's book of life (21:27); and the throne of God and the Lamb is in the midst of the city. Clearly the presence of God and the Lamb is that which makes the new city a place of paradise and joy.

Thus R structurally or literarily stresses the Lordship of Christ. The apocalypse begins and ends with the statement that Christ is alpha and omega, the eternal Lord, and each of the four visions stresses some aspect of Christ's Lordship. Further, the title, "Lamb" (Greek: ἀρνίον [*arnion*]) for Christ is the controlling term throughout R. It appears no less than twenty eight times and is a continual reminder of Christ's victory through his sacrificial death.[31] Sometimes R speaks of the Lamb that was slain, sometimes the blood of the Lamb, sometimes the conquering Lamb. Each term is roughly synonymous since the Lamb has won victory through his atoning death. Finally, R dramatizes Christ's Lordship by the hymns sung to him. R has several liturgical sections in which heavenly choirs sing to both God and the Lamb. There are three hymns to the Lamb in R chapter 5, two in 7, one in 11, one in 12, one in 15, and one in 19. These hymns form a dramatic pause in the events of R during which the events are interpreted and thus they highlight the centrality of Christ in world history, judgment, and eternity.

[31] In R 5:6, 8, 12, 13; 6:1, 16; 7:9, 10, 14, 17; 12:11; 13:8, 11; 14:1, 4, 10; 15:3; 17:14; 19:7, 9; 21:9, 14, 22, 23, 27; 22:1, 3.

R is then a highly Christocentric book. Although AP clearly is also a Christian apocalypse written by a pious person who worshipped Christ as Lord, its fascination with the place of the dead, both in hell and paradise overshadows any Christological emphasis. For John the most important consideration connected with the end of the age is that Christ, the Lord of Lords, the Lamb that was slain, will be there towering over the cosmos and history, giving judgment to Satan and his minions and joy to the saints.

7. Conclusions

First of all it is fairly clear that despite the growing dislike of millenarianism in the early church, the strong traditions about the inspiration of R insured that it would be accepted eventually. Early scholars such as Dionysius of Alexandria, Origen, and Eusebius were very suspicious of millennial teaching (probably because of Montanism and because heretics such as Cerinthus maintained it). Yet Origen affirmed the inspiration of R and Eusebius had to admit that the church generally accepted it as canonical. This situation contrasts with AP which was rather harmonious with the ascetic spirit of the age in its gruesome picture of sinners in hell yet had only local support for canonicity (in Egypt and perhaps in Palestine). Thus in spite of the taste some Christians had for this sort of literature, the tradition about inspiration for this apocalypse was too weak. This fact also explains the much weaker textual support for AP.

Second, AP began a trajectory that would influence several later Christian apocalypses such as Apocalypse of Ezra, Vision of Ezra, Apocalypse of Paul, Apocalypse of the Virgin, Sibylline Oracles II, and even Dante's medieval work, *The Inferno*. There remained in the church a certain tendency among some people to be fascinated with viewing, by means of reading these texts, the torment of sinners in hell.

Third, R was more than just an apocalypse with some esoteric knowledge of the throne room of God in heaven or the abode of the dead or even of the future. Rather R is a profound statement about the Lordship of Jesus Christ, the Lord of the church, of history, of the cosmos, and of eternity. R sets the tone for the book when it begins with Christ's statement that he is the alpha and omega. This tone continues until he restates this in the last chapter. In between, Christ the slain Lamb bestrides history conquering foes and saving his elect. The term Lamb (ἀρνίον [*arnion*]) in reference to Christ appears in R no less than twenty-eight times. It is the controlling concept for most scenes in the book. The Revelation of John is philologically, literarily, liturgically (the hymns), and theologically Christocentric.

The answer to our question, "Why was R accepted into the canon and not AP?" seems to be twofold. First, the traditions concerning the authority and inspiration of R were stronger and more universal. Second, the Christocentric message of R made it a considerable contributor to the church's theology of Christ the *pantokratôr*.

CHAPTER 12

Approaching the Millennial Issue with Ministry in Mind

VIRGIL WARREN

In regard to the end times, we do well to learn a lesson from Jewish religious leaders of Jesus' day. They had so exactly worked out their understanding of Messianic prophecy that they did not even recognize the Messiah when he came. Of course, we will not be *that* wrong this time. We will not fail to recognize him because his return will not be a local, private entrance into the human sphere (Matt 24:23–27). Nevertheless, we need to hold loosely to our expectancies about the time of that event, about its relationship to other future events, and about the very nature of those related events.

The nature of the millennium and the millennial reign of Revelation 20 is a prime example of this last point. Christians have long differed over whether that reign is a political one on earth that will last—perhaps approximately—a thousand years, or whether "kingdom" and "thousand years" figuratively refer to the church and its lengthy existence, the reign being in heaven. The second option, "amillennialism," means that there is no distinct period of time or manner of divine operation in the world aside from the church established in Acts 2 and commissioned in Matthew 28.

The first option has several variants differing according to the kingdom's chronological relationship to Christ's return. "Postmillennialism" says that his coming follows the millennium. It is a "golden age" ushered in by mankind's positive response to Christian proclamation. In general, postmillennialism envisions a process in which human affairs improve until at some point in history the millennial kingdom comes in through the power of truth and influence.

"Premillennialism" pictures an opposite scenario in which world conditions worsen until Christ comes to accomplish by *force* what *influence* alone did not do. In addition, some formulations of this schematic have the millennium in turn preceded by a "tribulation," a seven-year period of intense evil. In connection with that era, Christ's followers take part in a "rapture," which takes them out of the world before, after or during the tribulation. The Lord himself establishes the long-awaited kingdom and rules a thousand years, on earth, in Jerusalem, over a kingdom that replaces the kingdoms of this world.

The question arises as to which of these formats the history of God's work on earth will follow. We wonder why equally committed Christians should have such divergent understandings if in fact scripture presents a reasonably clear picture of these occurrences. The differences are surely not due to differing commitments to the truth and authority of the Bible or to differing intelligence of interpreters. It is more likely that the variations reflect differing assumptions about the way human language operates in the Bible, varying circumstances in which Christians do their interpreting, and personality differences that affect expectancies about the very nature of truth itself. In general, such differences come from hermeneutics, environment, and personality.

As to the impact of environment on this topic, it is instructive to note that *amillennialism* flourished during the time when there was a union of church and state: in general, from the time of Augustine onward. Church-state union fosters satisfaction with the status quo and does not prompt the interpreter to look for something better inasmuch as the church and God's people already enjoy a favored status. *Postmillennialism* flourished in the nineteenth century, a period of apparent progress and relative peace on a worldwide scale. Optimism about man and the future fits with an improving world situation that eventuates in the millennium. With the coming of World War I, the rise of communism, the Great Depression in America, World War II, the Korean Conflict, Vietnam, etc., postmillennialism has fallen out of favor more and more. In this same time frame, *premillennialism* has become increasingly popular, presumably because a deteriorating world climate corresponds with the expected historical pattern preceding Christ's return. In interpreting passages related to the millennial question, Christians run the risk of having their expectancies unconsciously influenced by their situation in the world. That phenomenon is what crystallized the Jews' anticipation of a political Messianic figure; they quite understandably yearned for relief from foreign domination by a pagan power.

Each person must decide how to deal with the millennial question. From a practical standpoint the best course of actions seems to be as follows: *tentatively take an amillennial position, fulfill the responsibilities assigned to us in the church age, and wait to see whether something comes that is more tangible than the present "spiritual" kingdom.* If God inaugurates something more, well and good; if not, nothing is lost. It is unwise to *deny* what *God* will do in the *future*; it is also unwise to affirm more than his previous revelation clearly teaches. Several considerations commend this course of action.

(1) *Amillennialism makes a lesser claim* about the kingdom than the other views do. The church as a spiritual entity is basically within the other views. Even in the Old Testament period when the kingdom had a political component, the spiritual kingdom within it—spiritual Israel, the remnant—was in fact the more important component (Rom 9:6). Similarly the church equals the "spiritual" component of any political kingdom Christ might later establish. Claiming less about future world events concentrates our ministries on the present spiritual aspect of Christ's reign, which is naturally the important part anyway.

(2) *How we live and what we do meantime are the same under all three formats.* Sometimes premillennialists are accused of not trying adequately to work through social structures to alleviate social concerns, because they tend to see these structures as evil and therefore ineffective for correcting social ills. Instead, proclaiming salvation to individuals is the only way to bring lasting improvement. But lack of social action need not follow from this millennial viewpoint.

Postmillennialists are sometimes accused of thinking that they can bring in the kingdom by their own effort through social and political means, which in the extreme could degenerate into the social gospel and liberationist theology. But again such extremes need not represent the mentality or *modus operandi.* How we understand the millennial kingdom could affect Near Eastern foreign policy because dispensational premillennialism tends to connect events in that area with the favored status of Israel in God's long-range plan. Our personal living, relationships, and ministry of edification and outreach proceed unaffected.

(3) *A "wait-and-see" approach encourages Christian unity.* There are so many inescapable controversies that divide us and divert our energy, time and resources away from Christian life and mission. They are inescapable because they deal with acts to be performed. But in the interests of unity we can put on hold our understanding of eschatological events that do not affect present "doing" as long as we affirm in principle the truthfulness of what scripture means where we do not understand it completely. Adopting a broader platform means, so to speak, that more people can stand on it. We can then more easily present a united testimony to people who do not even understand that Christ came the first time.

(4) *The purpose of prophecy is to create hope for the triumph of good over evil*, not to write history ahead of time. Being assured of future triumph gives us sufficient encouragement to persevere in the face of present adversity even when visible indicators bode failure for what we espouse. Jesus told his disciples it was not for them to know the times and seasons the Father keeps within his own authority (Acts 1:7). The time of his return the Lord himself did not know during his incarnation (Matt 24:36). *When* things will happen or exactly *how* they will take place is not necessary for faithfully fulfilling present responsibilities. What matters is that the outcome is not in doubt. The clear teachings Christians confess together include the personal, visible, unpredictable return of Christ for his people worldwide; the resurrection of the dead, judgment to come; and the final, permanent separation of good from evil. More than these things are not necessary for strengthening and extending the reign of Christ now.

(5) *Neither Jesus nor his disciples conformed to first-century expectations for a national kingdom.* Consequently, for the time being it is sensible to make minimum affirmation about events beyond the church era. The essential issue is whether Old Testament predictions of the Messianic kingdom were meant to be literal or analogous. Jesus' main controversy with the Pharisees came from his refusal to identify with their anticipations of a national kingdom. Paul's conflicts with the Judaizing teachers were also caused by his refusal to present the Messianic king-

dom as an aspect of political Israel. Arguing for such a kingdom in the end times may amount to just one more attempt to satisfy our "hankering" after a political expression of the kingdom of God. In the New Testament all Old Testament predictions of the kingdom are treated as fulfilled in what Jesus established on Pentecost. Therefore, in what God has said and done so far through Christ, there is no positive basis for expecting anything more about the kingdom than what God has already set up. Toward this endeavor we direct our ministries wholeheartedly.

Of course, we can imagine that a spiritual phase of the kingdom would precede its political dimension either because God intended to inaugurate the whole thing in two phases or because he postponed the second phase when the Jews rejected his Son at his first coming. Nevertheless, Paul argues that even the Mosaic law and national Israel were secondary elements in God's operation as shown by the fact that they came later than the promise (Gal 3:15–25). Grace-faith preceded law-nation; interpersonal preceded legal; spiritual preceded physical. So the former is more basic than the latter. The Old Testament system was a "parable" (Heb 9:9) and shadow (Heb 10:1) of later realities. It was not the same kind of thing, but a preceding material analogy to a subsequent spiritual reality.

When the perfect is come the imperfect is removed (1 Cor 13:10). When the former is taken away, it is not reinstated (Heb 7:18–19; 8:13; etc.). The Mosaic law (Jer 31:31–34; Heb 8–10), its priesthood (Ps 110:4; Heb 5–7), its basis for salvation (Ps 40:6–8; Heb 10), its temple—in short, the whole system—was secondary, not final. Messiah's work having begun in spirit-interpersonalism-grace/faith, we need not expect a return to flesh-law-nation (Gal 3:3) in order to have God's ideal situation. Circumcision and Israelite citizenship are not antithetical to grace-faith (Rom 3:31), but they are not necessary to it. The supremacy and finality of the spiritual does not *disprove* the possibility of a separate earthly kingdom. It does remove the material aspect as a positive expectancy on the basis of principle. The lack of a positive basis for expectancy has to be provided for by clearer predictions than those we seem to have in either testament.

This line of thought is reinforced by the fact that there can be only one universal eternal kingdom like the one anticipated in Psalm 89;

Daniel 2:34–35, 42; 7:13–14 (cf. Isa 9:7). There could be several parallel eternal kingdoms and several sequential universal kingdoms, but there can be only one universal eternal kingdom of a given sort. Therefore, all Old Testament prophecies about a future kingdom refer to the same kingdom, Messiah's kingdom; and Messiah has only one kingdom, the one that the New Testament says he has already established. A return to what includes a political, fleshly, national, legal, material kingdom after faith-grace has come does not have to happen to satisfy Old Testament prophecy in its intended sense. Such a kingdom would seem to be a second kingdom, one nearly as different from the church as Israel was.

A common belief is that at this first coming Jesus would have established a church-state kingdom if the Jews had accepted him. Since they did not, he instituted only its spiritual component on an interim basis, making the church a "parenthesis" in the long-term scheme. A major observation excludes such an idea: *the Jews rejected Jesus precisely because he did not offer them a political kingdom*. The interpersonal nature of his heavenly kingdom presented the stumbling block for them during his ministry. Many of their specific objections to his Messianic claims were facets of this one major difficulty. He even said that his kingdom was not of this world; it was not one that could be established the way this world's kingdoms are established—by military force (John 18:36). To suppose that he would have initiated a church-state system had the Jews accepted him forgets that they did not accept him because he refused to do that very thing. This consideration looks away from distinguishing the millennial kingdom from the church.

A wait-and-see approach frees us to acknowledge five elements in Revelation 20 that may tell against it. First (1) *Satan is said to be bound during the millennium* (20:3, 7), which precedes his final judgment and overthrow (20:10). If the millennium equals the church age, he is bound now. Inasmuch as evil still exists in the world, we wonder what it would mean for him to be bound.

One possibility is that (a) in principle Satan has been bound by the work of Christ. His doom is sealed by the cross and resurrection. In other words, Satan is potentially bound now. That potential is realized and individualized as people accept the gospel. The emphasis here is on salvation from *the power of sin*, that is, from consequences that can be reversed by reconciliation. The binding-loosing imagery in Mathew 16:19; 18:18 may refer to proclamation. If binding-loosing amounts to locking-unlocking, other passages come into view as well (Rev 1:8; 3:7; 9:14; cf. Job 12:14; Isa 22:22). The gospel, however, is not bound (2 Tim 2:9). In effect Satan is as good as vanquished. His binding, which is potential for all, is actualized in individuals who believe.

A related option is that (b) demonic possession contrary to the will of the possessed can now be overcome by the power of Christ anywhere. Those who returned from the mission of the seventy rejoiced because even demons were subject to them in Jesus' name. The Lord responded that he had seen Satan fall like a star from heaven (Luke 10:17–18). Satan's supernatural stranglehold on humanity was being broken by Messiah's greater power. Demon possession is still possible during the church age, but exorcism through Christ is possible for people in any nation. Previously it may have been available only among the Jews. The emphasis here is on deliverance from the *power of Satan*. While both of these suggestions may be true in themselves, neither may correspond to what the binding of Satan means in Revelation 20.

Not only is he bound during the millennium, but (2) *Satan's binding is something reversed temporarily after the millennium*. If the binding of Satan refers to potential *salvation* available through Christ, the loosing of Satan would apparently imply a time when the gospel is not effective or available. That does not seem likely. If binding him refers to divine *power* to conquer demonic power, loosing him would indicate a brief time when Christ's power would not be effective, available, or used for this purpose. Again that does not seem likely. These two factors look away from individualizing and "potentializing" the binding of Satan.

(3) *During the thousand years Satan is not deceiving the nations*. Obviously Satan *is* deceiving the nations now in some sense, in some respects, to some extent. We could say that in the gospel Satan's deception is *potentially* broken because now there is a universal alternative to his influence. Previously, during the Jewish dispensation God allowed the other nations to walk in their own ways (Acts 14:15–27; 17:30). It goes without saying that the actual effectiveness of the gospel is conditioned on its availability and free-will acceptance, two provisos not addressed by the binding-loosing imagery because of limitations of the im-

agery itself. The "potential" approach, however, runs into difficulty again with the reversal of the binding. That would mean, not just the unavailability of the gospel later, but its ineffectiveness as well.

Perhaps the point is that Satan *himself* can no longer *directly* deceive. Evil influences and personnel—both human and demonic and already present in the first century—God allows to play themselves out to whatever extent they can do so on their own. Satan himself cannot bring new factors into the situation. All the while, however, he is still the "god of this world" (2 Cor 4:4; cf. Eph 2:2; 1 John 4:4; 5:19) even though he is "cast out" (John 12:31) and judged (John 16:11).

A fourth element of description is that (4) *during the millennium previous martyrs live/come-to-life and reign with Christ*, a situation defined as "the first resurrection" (20:5). The text does not say where the reigning takes place, but it occurs before "the rest of the dead" resurrect/live-again. Presumably this refers to the martyrs' intermediate state while earth history is still going on, because at the end of this time there are people on earth for Satan to deceive when he is let go. "The rest of the dead" could include everyone besides martyrs, that is, both the evil dead and the righteous dead who were not killed for their faith. Conceivably the unmartyred dead, however, may not be excluded if the text simply intends to encourage people faced with the possibility of martyrdom. "Martyrs" could represent both a fact and a mentality—those who actually endured it and others who would have if it had been necessary. Another picture of dead Christians during the intermediate state (Rev 6:9–11) seems to use "martyrs" to stand for all the faithful, because they are told to rest till the other martyrs have fulfilled their course. During that time non-martyrs would be dying in the faith as well.

Since the church has actually existed for nearly two millennia, (5) *"a thousand years" has to be taken figuratively in an amillennial format.* One rationale for taking it to mean simply a long time is that (a) the context in which "a thousand years" stands is highly figurative. If other elements are so figurative, this number may also be figurative. (b) Elsewhere in Revelation numbers do—or in all likelihood do—have a figurative import: the twelve thousand from each of the twelve tribes, the seven spirits of God, etc.

On a play-it-safe policy, we may suppose that during the church age Satan does not himself directly operate in the ongoing deception of the nations/Gentiles. Evil influences that originated with him and evil persons who get their inspiration from him still carry out that work. But the gospel of Christ and the power of Christ are currently sufficient to protect anyone against the results of sin and the power of demons. In that practical sense Satan is potentially bound for everyone and actually bound for Christians. In principle and in effect, Satan is as good as defeated because he is actually being overthrown and will be completely and permanently overthrown after he is allowed to use his influence and power directly for a time. If there is a separate age, however, in which the devil's bondage is greater than it is now, we will be perfectly free to rejoice over that fact when it happens.

But the important thing here is not whether these suggestions answer at least five difficulties in Revelation 20 we can pose against our own proposal. The important thing is that on this subject we can afford to be wrong in this way. If amillennialism errs, it is not so much that it is wrong as that it is not right enough. Not only are its ideas about Revelation 20 admittedly true—even if they are not the true ones the Revelator intended; they are included in the other, more elaborate millennial reconstructions.

We can hold on to our view tentatively more than tenaciously because millennial views do not have distinctive behavioral correlates. We do not have to "defend it to the death" nor disprove the alternatives. In interpretation generally, we do not have to be right about everything that in theory scripture does sufficiently reveal, but we need to be right about the ones that have implications for life and service. Try as we might, there is no way to avoid facing some subjects head on, because we have to decide what to *do*, and we have to decide what to do *now*. The only recourse to being wrong about those matters is through the grace of forgiveness by him who acknowledges the integrity of the heart (cf. Ps 19:14). But on the millennial question we do not have to depend on even that.

A provisional amillennial stance avoids the division that attempting to be more correct on this question seems inevitably to foment. All the while, people of all persuasions—including this one—still benefit from the principal purpose of all predictive prophecy: they gain the hope that comes from knowing the triumph of good over evil, and that hope supplies sufficient motivation to remain *faith*ful till we all can really *see* (2 Cor 5:7). Meanwhile, we are thoroughly furnished for all Christian morality and ministry.

CHAPTER 13

Living the Double Life: Revealing Revelation's Paradoxes

AMANDA SMITH

Throughout Revelation, John creates paradoxes to express the double-sided nature of the life of a Christian. It is a message which reminds us that for God's people, all is not as it seems. We seem to be overcome and yet we are overcomers.

In Revelation 1:18 and 5:6, Jesus is depicted as dead but alive, and throughout the remainder of the book, we see that the same is true of his followers.

In 6:9–11 we meet the martyrs under the altar. Like their Lord, they have been slain but are alive. Their pain is real yet it has not overwhelmed them. As we continue through Revelation, we come to the sweet and bitter scroll in chapter 10:9–10. In John's mouth it is sweet as honey and yet it makes his stomach bitter. John reminds his reader that there are two sides to his message: the sweet and the bitter, the peace and the pain. Our pain is not removed and yet we have peace, comfort and strength. In chapter 11 we find another paradox. We are introduced to the two martyrs. They seem invincible: they are "the two lampstands that stand before the Lord of the earth. And if anyone desires to harm them, fire proceeds out of their mouth and devours their enemies; and if anyone would desire to harm them, in this manner he must be killed" (11:4–5 NASB). And yet they are clothed in sackcloth; they are familiar with mourning. Anyone unfamiliar with the paradoxes of Revelation would be surprised to see that these two witnesses are killed by the beast that comes up out of the abyss. But we are not. We know that all is not as it seems. They are hurt, but God protects them from ultimate destruction. John continues this theme in chapter 12, where we find a woman in labor and a huge, red dragon poised to devour her child. She and her child are extremely vulnerable and yet they are unharmed. At the last minute the child is caught up to God and the woman is whisked away to a place of safety in the wilderness. In the same way as the sweet but bitter scroll, the dead but living martyrs and the crushed yet invincible witnesses, this woman reminds us of the two sides of our experience. We are dead yet living, crushed yet overcoming, vulnerable and yet saved. Our lives are sweet yet bitter. This message reveals to us that suffering in life does not mean God is not with us. Suffering is a normal part of the Christian's existence. Our hope is in freedom from this suffering in the next life and in the God who is waiting to welcome us into his arms.

In class with Mr. Friskney we explored these paradoxes, but I was fascinated to find them in life outside of the classroom as well. As I have come across signs of these paradoxes in life, I have collected them to encourage me in times when the dark side of the paradox is all I see. It is a reminder that I am not alone in my struggles. This anthology is a collection of prose, poems and hymn lyrics, some my own writings and some quotes from other authors, which reveal these paradoxes in life. The collection brings together writers from different times, places and walks of life. This is a testimony to our shared experience of the double life.

1. Mourning yet Singing I

My life flows on in endless song;
Above earth's lamentation
I hear the sweet though far off hymn
That hails a new creation:
Through all the tumult and the strife
I hear the music ringing;
It finds an echo in my soul—
How can I keep from singing?

What though my joys and comforts die?
The Lord my Savior liveth;
What though the darkness gather round!
Songs in the night He giveth:
No storm can shake my inmost calm

While to that refuge clinging;
Since Christ is Lord of heaven and earth,
How can I keep from singing?

I lift mine eyes; the cloud grows thin;
I see the blue above it;
And day by day this pathway smoothes
Since first I learned to love it:
The peace of Christ makes fresh my heart,
A fountain ever springing:
All things are mine since I am His—
How can I keep from singing?[1]

2. Suffering yet Joyful

Recently I gave birth to my first child. During labor, I had a strange experience. As each contraction surged, I heard a phrase in my mind: "Joy comes in the morning." I knew I'd heard it somewhere before but couldn't remember where. The important thing was that it helped me through the pain because it was a reminder that, although it was difficult, it wasn't pointless: when the pain was over, I'd have a beautiful little girl. Joy would come in the morning. It somehow made the pain more bearable. Afterwards I found the phrase in Psalm 30:4–5. It says:

> Sing to the Lord, all you godly ones! Praise his holy name. His anger lasts for a moment, but his favor lasts a lifetime! Weeping may go on all night, but joy comes with the morning. (New Living Translation)

After thinking more about this passage, I realized that this relates to more than just my birth pains. It relates to all of life and the pain and struggles we face. To continue the story of child birth, I wouldn't have been able to enjoy my daughter if the pain had made me give up. But it's ridiculous to imagine a woman in labor giving up because it is too pain-

[1] Robert Lowry, 1860. See *The Cyber Hymnal*, www.tch.simplenet.com/htm/h/howcanik.htm.

ful. She has hope of things to come. Of course, just as labor leaves the mother exhausted, we sometimes come through trials feeling exhausted, tormented, even emotionally and spiritually wrecked. Enduring doesn't mean pretending everything is okay. Enduring doesn't mean always feeling close to God. It means continuing to be faithful to God even when He seems far away. We can do this because we have hope of things to come: an eternal life with our Father.

I have a photo which was taken a minute after I delivered. In one way it is the worst photo of me I have ever seen. My hair is everywhere. My eyes are red. My skin is blotchy. And yet in another way it is a beautiful photo because I am glowing with happiness as I hold my newborn daughter. It is obvious from the photo that I have been through much pain and hard work and yet at the same time I have such joy. This is the face of every Christian. We weep yet sing. We are slain yet living. We are weak yet strong. We are overcome yet victorious. We have this strange combination of suffering and joy at the same time. Our suffering is real yet we are able to see beyond it to the joy of heaven. To remember the verse from Psalms, our night is long and the weeping seems endless but the morning is never far away! Joy *will* come in the morning.

3. Tormented yet Peaceful

When peace like a river attendeth my way,
When sorrows like sea billows roll;
Whatever my lot,
Thou hast taught me to say,
"It is well, it is well with my soul."

Though Satan should buffet, tho' trials should come,
Let this blest assurance control,
That Christ has regarded my helpless estate,
And hath shed His own blood for my soul."[2]

[2] Horatio G. Spafford, "It Is Well with My Soul," from *The Hymnal for Worship and Celebration* (Waco, Texas: Word Music, 1986) number 493.

4. Wanting to Curse yet Blessing

No Grass Grows[3]

I roam where no grass will grow,
The bees make no honey,
The cows are dry.
At night the moon withholds her borrowed light;
By day the sun is shrouded in dark clouds,
The wheat and barley wither on the stalk,
Fruits shrivel before they ripen.
God has withdrawn his blessings.
He has decided to test my faith.
Will I continue to love and trust him
Even in this bleak, harsh wilderness?
He does not bless me,
I want to curse him.
Let my curses melt into blessings.

5. Terrified yet Perseverant

And when you're alone, there's a very good chance
You'll meet things that scare you right out of your pants.
There are some, down the road between hither and yon,
That can scare you so much you won't want to go on.
But on you will go
Though the weather be foul.
On you will go
Though your enemies prowl.
On you will go
Though the Hakken-Kraks howl.
Onward up many a frightening creek,
Though your arms may get sore
And your sneakers may leak.
On and on you will hike.

---

[3] Robert Van De Weyer, *Celtic Praise: Daily Prayers and Blessings* (Nashville: Abingdon Press, 1998) 40.

And I know you'll hike far
And face up to your problems
Whatever they are. . .
And will you succeed?
Yes! You will indeed
(98 and 3/4 percent guaranteed.)
Kid, you'll move mountains![4]

6. *Laughing yet Crying*

To be both ironic and Christian is to know, with a knowing deeper than doctrine, the simple, unnerving truth that the visage of faith is not the happy face but the masks of comedy and tragedy, alternating, unpredictably, between laughter and tears, sometimes crying and laughing at the same time, or even, on occasion, crying because it's so funny and laughing because it hurts so much.[5]

7. *Wandering yet Found*

All that is gold does not glitter,
Not all those who wander are lost;
The old that is strong does not wither,
Deep roots are not reached by the frost.
From the ashes a fire shall be woken,
A light from the shadows shall spring;
Renewed shall be blade that was broken,
The crownless again shall be king.[6]

---

[4] Dr. Seuss, *Oh, The Places You'll Go!* (New York: Random House, 1990).

[5] Patrick Henry, *The Ironic Christian's Companion: Finding the Marks of God's Grace in the World* (New York: Riverhead Books, 2000) 7.

[6] J. R. R. Tolkien, *The Fellowship of the Ring* (New York: Ballantine Books, 1990) 231.

8. Doubting yet Believing

February 17, 1993: In class today Mr. Friskney talked about trials. He said that a trial is anything that challenges my faith and my relationship with God. This has given me a new way of seeing doubt. Doubt challenges my faith. If I view it as a trial, I see that the attack is external, not internal. We all have doubts in our relationship with God, but what matters is whether we allow them to take hold, whether we allow our lives to be lived according to them. I can relate to the man who said to Jesus, "I believe, forgive my unbelief." I doubt yet I live in belief. I live as if I am in God's presence even if I don't feel Him there. Doubt and belief are constantly at war in me yet I know that I will emerge "the believing kind."

9. Losing All yet Thanking God

If everything is lost, thanks be to God
If I must see it go, watch it go,
Watch it fade away, die
Thanks be to God that He is all I have
And if I have Him not, I have nothing at all
Nothing at all, only a farewell to the wind
Farewell to the grey sky
Goodbye, God be with you evening October sky.
If all is lost, thanks be to God,
For He is He, and I, I am only I.[7]

10. Feeling Forsaken yet Obeying

Do not be deceived, Wormwood. Our cause is never more in danger than when a human, no longer desiring, but still intending, to do our Enemy's will, looks round upon a universe from which every

[7] Sheldon Vanauken, *A Severe Mercy* (San Francisco: Harper and Row, 1987). Poem by Dom Julian, a friend of the author. It was kept at the bedside of the author's wife as she lay dying.

trace of Him seems to have vanished, and asks why he has been forsaken, and still obeys.[8]

11. Mourning yet Singing II

Suzanne was an only child, so her cousin was the closest thing to a sister she had. Yesterday had started with such excitement as her cousin rushed to the hospital to deliver her third child but the day had ended in grief. The cousin contracted a frightening illness and suddenly her body was transformed from lifegiver to lifeless. The tiny new baby would begin life without his mother. My friend was devastated.

Today I find it difficult to focus on the preacher as my mind drifts to Suzanne and her grief. She's usually late and I can always tell when she arrives because I can hear her sweet voice high over the congregation. I've often thought it's the way I imagine an angel might sing: high but strong and pure, totally unaffected. As we stand to sing, I am comforted again by the sound of her voice among all the others. I am taken again to the throne room of God as all his saints lift their voices to praise him. I turn to see my friend singing with all her heart, praising her Father. And yet today something is different. Today her face is wet with tears and I know she is pleading for God to hold her cousin close to him and wishing she could do it herself. And yet her voice is unwavering. I watch my friend experience the pain and peace all at once and long for the day when he will wipe every tear from our eyes. The tears and pain and grief will pass away but the singing will continue, eternally.

12. Grieving yet Dancing

"There is a time for everything, a season for every activity under heaven.…a time to cry and a time to laugh. A time to grieve and a time to dance" (Eccl 3:1, 4, New Living Translation).

---

[8] C. S. Lewis, *The Screwtape Letters* (New York: Macmillan, 1982) 39. Screwtape is a devil, writing to a lesser devil and advising him how to lead astray a human, thus "our Enemy" is God.

13. Epilogue

Most of the paradoxes in Revelation are in chapters 1–12. As we continue to read Revelation, after chapter 12 the paradoxes become less frequent because God is overcoming the painful half of our experience. As we see in 21:3–4, "He shall wipe away every tear from their eyes; and there shall no longer be any death; there shall no longer be any mourning, or crying or pain; the first things have passed away" (NASB). We will no longer be dead yet living, crushed yet overcoming, vulnerable yet saved. We will simply be living, overcoming and saved. Amen! Come, Lord Jesus!